Communication Skills for Project and Programme Managers

London: TSO

information & publishing solutions

Published by TSO (The Stationery Office) and available from:

Online
www.tsoshop.co.uk

Mail, Telephone, Fax & E-mail
TSO
PO Box 29, Norwich, NR3 1GN
Telephone orders/General enquiries: 0870 600 5522
Fax orders: 0870 600 5533
E-mail: customer.services@tso.co.uk
Textphone 0870 240 3701

TSO Shops
16 Arthur Street, Belfast BT1 4GD
028 9023 8451 Fax 028 9023 5401
71 Lothian Road, Edinburgh EH3 9AZ
0870 606 5566 Fax 0870 606 5588

TSO@Blackwell and other Accredited Agents

The information contained in this publication is believed to be correct at the time of manufacture. Whilst care has been taken to ensure that the information is accurate, the publisher can accept no responsibility for any errors or omissions or for changes to the details given.

Melanie Franklin and Susan Tuttle have asserted their moral rights under the Copyright, Designs and Patents Act 1988, to be identified as the authors of this work.

The Swirl logo™ is a Trade Mark of the Office of Government Commerce

PRINCE2™ is a Trade Mark of the Office of Government Commerce

The PRINCE2 Cityscape logo™ is a Trade Mark of the Office of Government Commerce in the United Kingdom and other countries

PRINCE® is a Registered Trade Mark of the Office of Government Commerce in the United Kingdom and other countries

MSP™ is a Trade Mark of the Office of Government Commerce

A CIP catalogue record for this book is available from the British Library

A Library of Congress CIP catalogue record has been applied for

First published 2008

ISBN 9780113310821

Printed in the United Kingdom by The Stationery Office, London

N5810797 c20   06/08

Contents

List of figures

Acknowledgements

The ideas and content for this book are a result of our many years of experience in project and programme management. They are also a result of all the successes and failures we have had on our projects and programmes, and all of the stories and anecdotes we have collected over the years. However, we would specifically like to thank all of our colleagues, clients and associates whom we interviewed for this book (too numerous to mention), and Maurice Leppard and Lindsay Campbell for their many hours spent reading through the content.

REVIEWERS

Angela Berry	Information Services
Stuart Blackhurst	Assurant Solutions
Tony Levene	Quality Projects (Consulting) Ltd
Tim Reeks	HM Revenue & Customs
Edna Stewart	
Ajish Kurian Varghese	Petrofac
Stuart Wilson	National School of Government

MATURITY MARK

The TSO maturity mark on the back cover will help you decide if this publication is positioned at the appropriate level for your requirements and provide a route map to progress with embedding the OGC best-practice guidance. This publication, *Communication Skills for Project and Programme Managers*, is levels 2 and 3.

Level 2 is Repeatable (process discipline) – OGC guidance is used repeatedly.

Level 3 is Defined (institutionalized) – OGC guidance is defined/confirmed as a standard business process.

For more information on the TSO maturity mark and how it can help you, please visit www.best-management-practice.com

Introduction

1

1 Introduction

Communication is a constant in our lives – it takes place every moment of every day. So you would think we would be better at it!

The one thing guaranteed to get in the way of a successful project or programme is miscommunication.

Miscommunication – it's always the fault of the other party

- 'You never listen to anything I say'
- 'How can you have forgotten what I just told you'
- 'What part of "Don't start the test until all the users have signed in" did you not understand?'

In projects, miscommunication manifests itself in all routine problems:

- Suppliers not delivering on time (they did not 'hear' the importance of the delivery date)
- Users and members of the project team doing tasks in the wrong order (they did not 'understand' the plan)
- Duplication of work across the project team (they did not 'remember' who was supposed to be doing what work)
- Operational staff refusing to take part in testing (the project team did not 'listen' when the users said how busy they were).

These are just the 'official' problems. The 'unofficial' ones include the growing dislike of all your colleagues and the overwhelming desire to shut their fingers in a desk drawer whenever they walk into a room.

At its core, communication during a project is a process of managing stakeholders. Stakeholders include the team members as well as people outside the project who are affected by the project or its outcome. By managing these groups or individuals through effective communication, an environment of trust and collaboration can ensue. Without stakeholder buy-in, the project is doomed to contend with unnecessary misunderstandings, hardships and strained relationships. When people feel excluded from a process that directly impacts them, their well-being or their sense of security, they tend to resist cooperating with the offending party. However, without cooperation and support, the project could fail before it even starts.

Getting communication right requires effort and patience, but it is not difficult if we follow some simple principles. This publication gives an overview of these basic 'rules' of communication and shows how they can be applied to typical project and programme situations.

1.1 THE AUDIENCE FOR THIS PUBLICATION

This publication is for anyone who needs help getting their message across or understanding what is meant by the different messages they receive. The information is structured around a common project lifecycle and examines the different relationships and communication priorities of the main players in any project, including the sponsor, the project manager, the project team, the users, the suppliers and the audit or assurance function.

This publication forms part of a series of three publications, each highlighting a specific area of interpersonal skills demonstrated by effective project managers, programme managers and project and programme teams:

- Communication skills
- Leadership skills
- Team management skills.

The intended audience for these publications is not restricted solely to those already working in project or programme management, but includes anyone who is impacted by projects within their day-to-day work. However, a basic understanding of what a project is, and the organization structure that underpins projects and programmes, has been assumed.

1.2 THE STRUCTURE OF THIS PUBLICATION

A great deal of communication during a project is about relationship building, and formal project records and documents are created throughout its lifecycle. This publication explores how those relationships might best be developed, rather than providing a step-by-step guide to what should be written for each document template. Chapter 2 explores the basic mechanism that underpins any communication – sender, receiver, message – and describes the different preferences that people have for how the message is delivered. Chapter 3 examines the communication priorities as a typical project lifecycle unfolds.

The example case study used in this chapter is based on a typical project, involving internal and external suppliers and multiple stakeholders. However, even though the example is based on a standalone project, the ideas are valid for programmes and the projects that form those programmes. This is a practical guide, so at the start of each section of the lifecycle suggestions have been made for the types of message associated with each stage of a project and the likely audience for these messages.

Throughout the text, you will find advice and opinions from the project and programme managers interviewed for this book in boxes labelled 'Real world experience'. The quotes indicate new ideas, and sometimes illustrate how not to approach an issue.

Appendix A provides a detailed explanation of the most common methods of communication and how they can be applied to project and programme management.

1.3 WORKING WITHIN A PROJECT OR PROGRAMME MANAGEMENT ENVIRONMENT

A project is a temporary organization structure that is created to deliver outputs (products and services) that are justified on the basis that the benefits of having these outputs outweigh the cost of delivering them. Effective communication during the project is the responsibility of all the team members. The project manager will usually coordinate communication activities, such as setting up meetings, sending out notices or writing reports. However, every team member is responsible for ensuring that when they communicate about the project, their message has been received as intended and understood, even when dealing with each other.

A programme is a temporary organization structure that is created to coordinate and direct the implementation of a set of related projects and activities in order to deliver outcomes and benefits that will drive forward the achievement of an organization's strategy. The number of stakeholders increases enormously with a programme and thus the communication demands also increase. Effective communication between and among the numerous related projects is crucial. Many projects within the programme are dependent on each other; only when one finishes can another begin. The message of completion needs to be sent promptly and understood correctly in order for the timings to line up and resources to be used effectively. The size of the change associated with a programme means several stakeholders will need to be kept informed and consulted for longer periods of time. Extensive communication planning will need to be undertaken in a programme environment, though the principles are the same: to identify the stakeholders, understand their interests in the programme and keep them involved or informed depending on their needs.

To avoid repetition throughout the text, the terms project and project management have been used to represent activities and responsibilities that take place within a project or a programme environment.

The project and programme management terminology used in this book is based on the suite of guidance developed by the Office of Government Commerce (OGC), aimed at helping organizations manage projects and programmes. Principally, the terminology has been drawn from two approaches:

- PRINCE2™
- Managing Successful Programmes (MSP™).

Terminology from these approaches is included in the glossary at the end of this publication.

Figures 1.1–1.3 provide an overview of the links between the two approaches and the lifecycle model that is used in Chapter 3.

Figure 1.1 Getting started – overview of the links between PRINCE2, MSP and the lifecycle model

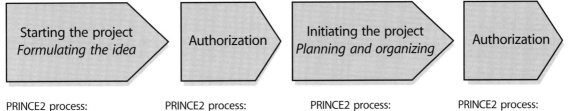

PRINCE2 process:
Starting up a Project
MSP Transformational Flow:
Identifying a Programme

PRINCE2 process:
Directing a Project
MSP Transformational Flow:
Approval to Proceed

PRINCE2 process:
Initiating a Project
MSP Transformational Flow:
Defining a Programme

PRINCE2 process:
Directing a Project
MSP Transformational Flow:
Approval to Proceed

Figure 1.2 Making progress – overview of the links between PRINCE2, MSP and the lifecycle model

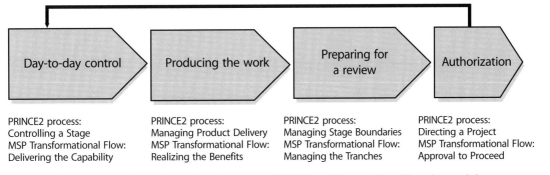

PRINCE2 process:
Controlling a Stage
MSP Transformational Flow:
Delivering the Capability

PRINCE2 process:
Managing Product Delivery
MSP Transformational Flow:
Realizing the Benefits

PRINCE2 process:
Managing Stage Boundaries
MSP Transformational Flow:
Managing the Tranches

PRINCE2 process:
Directing a Project
MSP Transformational Flow:
Approval to Proceed

Figure 1.3 Closing down – overview of the links between PRINCE2, MSP and the lifecycle model

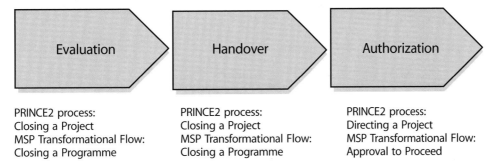

PRINCE2 process:
Closing a Project
MSP Transformational Flow:
Closing a Programme

PRINCE2 process:
Closing a Project
MSP Transformational Flow:
Closing a Programme

PRINCE2 process:
Directing a Project
MSP Transformational Flow:
Approval to Proceed

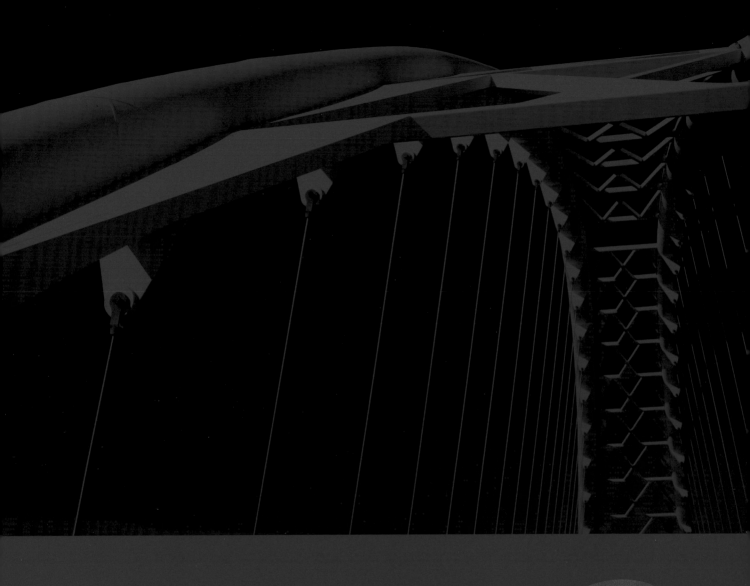

Definition and context of project and programme communication

2

2 Definition and context of project and programme communication

'Communication is the giving, receiving, processing and interpreting of information. Information can be conveyed verbally, non-verbally, actively, passively, formally, informally, consciously or unconsciously.'
(Project Management Body of Knowledge, Association for Project Management)

Information is sent in the form of messages created by the sender and understood by the receiver. The problem is that there is a space between the sender and the receiver, and this space can become filled with 'noise', i.e. misunderstandings, misinterpretations, prejudices and confusion. As shown in Figure 2.1, this space can affect the original message (from sender to receiver) and the reply (from receiver to sender).

Figure 2.1 Participants in communication

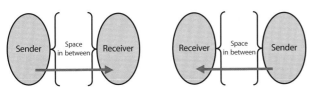

2.1 AIMS OF COMMUNICATION

The goal of communication is to ensure that the desired message is received and understood. The sender must be clear and open about the message, using language that can be understood by the receiver. The receiver has to be willing to hear or receive the message and the space in between should be conducive to communicating, which means there should be as little distortion of the original message as possible. In addition to minimizing the interferences, effective communication involves having a feedback mechanism in place, ensuring messages are

received correctly. By doing this, the receiver becomes the sender, confirming the message he or she received.

In a project or programme environment, the project teams, project managers and sponsors are sending information about the justification for the project, the vision of what it will create, the progress that is being made towards this vision, and the issues and changes that are getting in the way. Operational staff are sending information about what they need, when they need it and how they want to be involved in the project. In addition to these 'primary' stakeholders, other interests are represented by suppliers, customers, regulators and the community in which the organization operates, and, in some cases, the media.

2.2 OUTCOMES OF COMMUNICATION

Before undertaking any communication, consideration must be given to its outcome. The outcome is the result that you want to achieve or the conclusion that you want the receiver to draw from the information provided. In some cases, it is easier to start by identifying what outcome should not result from the communication. For example, when communicating with staff about the need for training in a new set of procedures, the desired outcome might be to reassure them that the training is straightforward and will not take very long. However, it is not the intention to make staff feel that the reason the training is so straightforward is because the project team does not think that staff are capable of anything too complicated. There are many situations in which multiple messages are being sent, and the overall outcome of these messages needs to be identified upfront, and the messages crafted to ensure that the outcome is achieved.

For example, consider a project or programme manager approaching their sponsor for extra funding to employ an administrator to support the project or programme. The possible (and sometimes unintentional) outcomes are as follows:

1 The sponsor appreciates how much work is involved and agrees to the request.

2 The sponsor agrees to the request but forms a negative opinion of the project or programme manager because the sponsor feels that the need for support should have been identified in the original budget, rather than being identified once the budget has been finalized.

3 The sponsor denies the request because he or she does not believe there is enough work to justify another staff member.

4 The sponsor denies the request because he or she believes the project or programme manager does not want to do the administration work themselves.

By identifying the desired outcome (option 1) and planning the method and message, the project or programme manager will increase their chances of success. Figure 2.2 illustrates the five key steps in planning any communication.

Another reason for carefully considering the outcome of a communication is that it enables the sender to be clear about the message they are sending – so they can get straight to the point and not waste the receiver's time with lots of extraneous information. We all know colleagues who never seem to get to the point, which makes them appear disorganized and unfocused.

Figure 2.2 Communication planning cycle

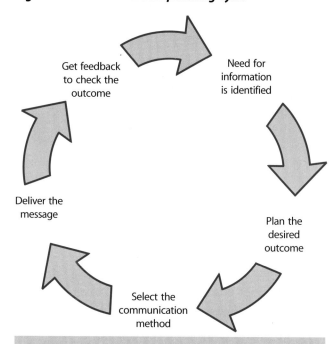

Need for information is identified

Plan the desired outcome

Select the communication method

Deliver the message

Get feedback to check the outcome

Real world experience

'I thought project managers were busy people, but the guy who manages projects in our office spends half his time giving updates. He tells me who is doing what, when they are doing it, who is on holiday, who is off on sick leave etc. when all I want to know is if the project is on time and on budget.'

2.3 RAPPORT – THE BASIS OF EFFECTIVE COMMUNICATION

In order to be able to communicate effectively, it is essential to establish a relationship between the sender and the receiver. For the 'primary' stakeholders, effort and time must be devoted to building this relationship. By developing a rapport, identifying common interests and shared views, distortion of the messages will be reduced, and the accuracy of the message that is sent and the message that is heard will be increased.

Building rapport requires the sender to understand the needs and views of the receiver, match the receiver's immediate needs, and only then introduce the real subject that they are trying to communicate. The easiest example of this 'pacing' technique is allowing the receiver to vent their feelings or get something off their chest before the sender starts speaking. Until this has taken place, the receiver is only thinking about what they want to say and they cannot hear the sender at all.

Rapport does not necessarily involve liking someone. This is important, because in business communications it is just not possible to like everyone with whom we have to communicate. Rapport is developing an understanding and showing empathy and acknowledgement of the other person's point of view. This does not mean agreeing with that point of view, or even liking it. By acknowledging the receiver's standpoint, it is possible to tailor the message so that they can hear it without the interference of their own views.

Developing rapport

In this section, we set out how to develop rapport, and in Chapter 3 we look at how this might be achieved with a range of different stakeholders.

Developing rapport involves:

- Taking time
- Being genuine
- Allowing the stakeholder to establish their views
- Inclusion of their communications style into your replies
- Introduction of your views into the conversation whilst still matching their communication style.

The first step in developing rapport is setting aside enough time to understand each of the stakeholders. Getting to understand what motivates and inspires others cannot be rushed, and may require a number of sessions before there is a 'breakthrough'. The speed at which rapport can be developed will be affected by how much common ground and common history there is between two parties. However, it is worth remembering that common history can be an advantage or a disadvantage, depending on whether there were conflicts or disagreements in the past.

The project or programme manager should demonstrate a genuine willingness to understand, and should not give the impression that this 'bonding' has been forced upon them. For example, setting up a meeting with one of your peers at a supplier company is not going to yield anything useful if you start the session by saying 'I know we have to have this meeting, but I want to make it clear, your firm works for me, and what I say goes.'

Allow the stakeholder to establish their views, even if this means talking about something that you consider irrelevant at this point in the project. If the stakeholder has a strong view about something, it is obviously important to them, and trying to putting it on hold until you are ready for it will make them frustrated. Instead of listening to your message, they will be thinking about what they want to say.

Watch and listen for signals about how the stakeholder prefers to communicate. For example, are they giving out lots of details, or are they giving an overview of the subject? Are there any favourite phrases or words that they use often? Are they speaking very slowly or very quickly? If possible, try to include some of their style in your reply, as they will respond to this and feel that you are the same as them.

Introduce the message that you need to communicate only once there is sufficient rapport. Now that you have developed a relationship, by matching the stakeholder's communications style, take the opportunity to use the style most appropriate to the message. For example, if the style so far has been fast paced and lively, with a discussion on light-hearted topics, slow your voice down and reduce the number of hand and arm waving gestures used, in order to convey a more serious topic that needs concentration. If, however, the stakeholder has shown anger or annoyance so far, consider lightening the tone to introduce a subject that demonstrates a benefit of the project, or an improvement that will result once the project has gone live.

It is not always possible to develop a close rapport with those with whom we communicate. In a project and programme environment, there are simply too many interested parties to be able to communicate one to one every time; therefore, communication has to be at a general level. However, there are ways in which even this general form of communication can be as targeted as possible. The sender must ensure that the message addresses all of the communication preferences of the possible receivers.

2.4 COMMUNICATION PREFERENCES

Each of us has a number of communication preferences, and they are a natural part of who we are and how we behave. However, they can be affected by the context of the situation, and we can display a number of preferences simultaneously. The preferences that are addressed in this publication are not an exhaustive list, but they cover the main requirements for effective communication:

- Sensory preferences
- Big picture and detail focused
- Options and procedures
- Negatives and positives
- Sameness and difference
- Internal conclusions or external validation.

Sensory preferences

Everyone has a primary sensory preference that governs how they like to give and receive information. Whilst the human body has five senses, those most relevant to business communications are: visionary (sight), auditory (hearing) and kinaesthetic (touch).

People who have a visionary preference will talk about 'seeing what we are doing', 'picturing the scene', 'visualising what happens next', and their ability to 'listen' might not be as strong as that of people with an auditory preference. They prefer to receive their information via diagrams, pictures, cartoons and symbols. They respond well to slides at a presentation as they like to 'see' information being presented to them.

People with an auditory preference talk about 'hearing what people are up to', listen to what is being said and may discard the other senses. Therefore, at a presentation, they may appear to be paying little attention as they are not looking at the presentation. However, this is because they are listening very carefully to what is being said, and the visuals are a distraction from this task.

People with a kinaesthetic preference will talk about 'feeling if something is right' or 'holding all of the responsibility'. Whilst they may receive their business communications via visual or auditory means, touch is important, so an opportunity to use a new product, rather than to look at the brochure for it or to listen to a speech about it, would be their preference.

Big picture and detail focused

One of the most common communication preferences is 'big picture' versus 'detail focused'. If the person you are communicating with is 'big picture', they will want to hear about the project in broad terms. They will disengage if they are given lots of detail, as they do not want to sift through it to find the important ideas and sentiments. In contrast, any communication that is too high level with not enough information will cause concern to those who are detail focused. They will be suspicious if they are not given the information that they feel they need to understand the whole situation.

In all communications, the simplest way to overcome the differences between these two preferences is to ensure that there is always a high-level summary, but that further details can be accessed at a later point. For example, in a presentation it is important to provide a high-level summary and a picture of the overall outcome, but setting out every single detail of how that will be achieved will not be relevant to all members of the audience.

Options and procedures

As part of the message, people who prefer to be given options will need an indication of what they are 'allowed' to do with the information – for example, including an opportunity for those with this preference to decide the order in which a number of activities should be carried out, or letting them choose from a list of recommendations the ones that should be implemented.

People with a 'procedures' preference need a step-by-step guide to what should be done, eradicating any choices for where to get started or what order to do things in.

Satisfying both preferences in the same audience can be tricky, but it can be done – for example, outlining all of the steps involved in testing a deliverable from the project, but concluding with an outline of two or three extra areas that the team member can choose to undertake, and decide where in the process to implement them.

Negatives and positives

Some people only feel comfortable discussing a subject once all the problems and difficulties that they are currently experiencing have been identified and understood. In other words, they have to start from the perspective of the problem and not the solution.

However, other people feel that this shot of 'negativity' at the start of any communication prevents them feeling positive enough to identify the solutions. They are solution focused, and for them, discussing how the situation will be better in the future is the only way to get started. Once this has been identified, they can think about how they might get there.

Although these are opposing views, it is possible to address both preferences in the same communication, by including pairs of statements, one from each perspective, followed by another pairing and then another, until all the needs have been met. This is more effective than trying to address the 'negatives' with all of the current problems and then addressing the 'positives' with all of the potential solutions. By the time you have met the needs of the negatives, the positives will have disengaged, and it will be difficult to recapture their attention and support.

Sameness and difference

The preference for sameness is about the reassurance or constraint that is provided by doing something very similar to what was done last time. However, those with a preference for difference feel that they have to do something different from what has gone before. Those with a preference for sameness feel threatened by this idea of stepping into the unknown, and they perform better if they feel that their work is based on previous experience and repetition.

Internal conclusions or external validation

Everyone has their own way of validating and endorsing what they have heard. For some, the importance, accuracy or usefulness of the information can only be judged once they have heard the views of their colleagues and friends. In other words, they draw their own ideas from the comparisons they make between their views and the views of others. Other people are internally focused, and can only make sense of a message once they have had a chance to think it through, compared it with other things that they know about or have heard of and drawn their own conclusions. They are unlikely to give immediate reactions to what they have heard. This does not mean that they are not in favour of the message, it is just that they have not processed it yet.

When communicating with internally focused people, it is important to consider the mechanism by which they can attain their quiet time. For example, do not push them for an immediate reaction but encourage them to come back to you at a mutually convenient time. When addressing those who are externally focused, consider including the views of others in the company, industry or community that the receiver respects, and demonstrate how others have used the information or taken action that will be helpful for the project.

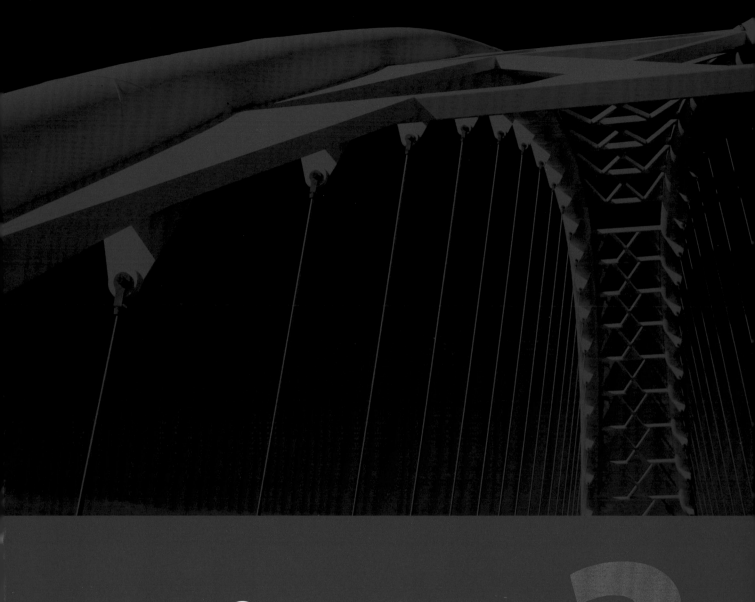

Communicating effectively in the project lifecycle

3

3 Communicating effectively in the project lifecycle

This chapter explains how communication is used throughout the project lifecycle. It highlights the key messages required at each stage in the project and discusses which methods would be best to convey them. To illustrate these points, a case study has been used throughout the chapter to bring the messages and methods to life.

The characteristics of the project in the case study are drawn from interviews conducted with many people involved in project and/or programme management and therefore are representative of a range of projects undertaken within an organization. The text is complemented by quotes from the interviewees, presented as 'Real world experience'.

Case study: the 'Next Biggest Thing' project

A small advertising agency (AdOne) specializing in television advertisements has recently been hired by High-Tech to produce a series of commercials about High-Tech's new software package that will rival the bigger, better-known players in the industry. The six commercials will introduce the company and product names to the public, building brand awareness and increasing sales.

AdOne has established a project team to design, film and edit the commercials. Senior managers and technical staff at High-Tech will work with the project team to provide product information and branding guidelines.

AdOne will use its partnership with TeleFilm Company to shoot the actual advertisements. Also, it will work with licensing and government bodies to ensure the commercials conform to regulatory standards.

Project stakeholders

Winning the business from High-Tech is a major coup for AdOne, as it has been interested in this client for a long time. As a result, the chief executive officer (CEO) has taken on the role of project sponsor. She will be supported in this role by the market research director as the senior user, who will represent the views of those who are in the market to buy High-Tech software. The AdOne advertising director and a senior manager from TeleFilm will advise on the capacity of the two organizations, resolve resourcing issues and settle any technical issues that arise during the project.

The project manager has been working at AdOne for a long time. She is highly experienced in creating new campaigns, and last year she worked on a similar campaign for another software supplier. She will be controlling the work of four teams (Figure 3.1):

- Design team – this is a group of young staff, and AdOne is their first employer. They have not worked for a client in the software industry before.
- Editing team – a small team of experienced editors, all of whom are working on multiple campaigns at any one time.
- High-Tech team – this team is formed of staff selected by High-Tech. However, the team members have no experience of how to brief an advertising agency.
- TeleFilm team – this team consists of a range of staff – from new graduates to those with experience of several hundred filming assignments. The manager of the Telefilm team is very experienced and has worked with AdOne before. However, he has not worked with this project manager.

Finally, there are several additional stakeholders who are interested in the project and its outcome of six television advertisements about the new, innovative technology.

The High-Tech programme incorporating the new project

This effort has been designed as a project within a programme at High-Tech, mainly because of its size, complexity and duration (Figure 3.2). As shown in Figure 3.3, the programme is formed of several related High-Tech projects offering breakthrough technology to everyday computer users. It is sponsored by the product development director, because the overall outcome of the programme is to introduce new technology. One of the business change managers will be the communications director, as several of the projects are related to the advertising campaign for these new products. The users for this aspect of the programme will be those seeing the advertising, including existing customers, potential customers, suppliers and competitors.

Figure 3.1 Stakeholders in the 'Next Biggest Thing' project

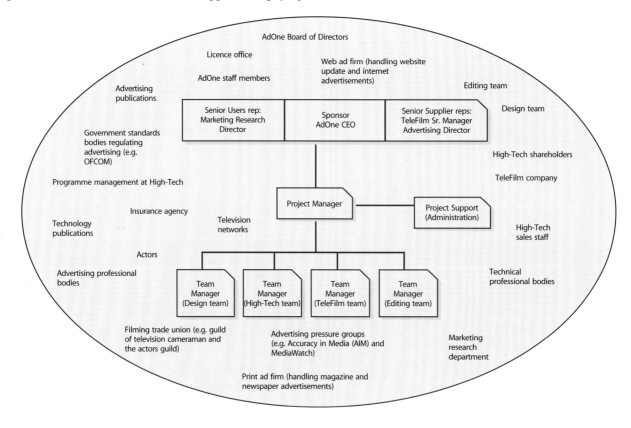

Figure 3.2 The High-Tech programme incorporating the 'Next Biggest Thing' project

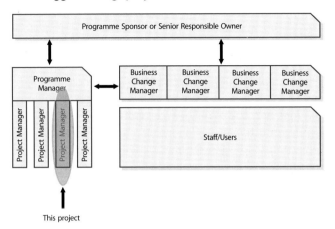

This project

Figure 3.3 The various projects forming one High-Tech programme

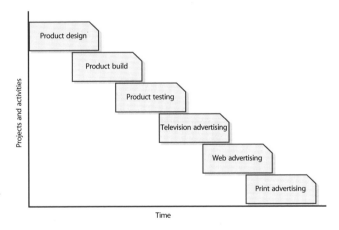

The projects in the programme involve designing and building the technology, testing it with users, and ensuring that it is compatible with mainstream software and hardware. Now that the technology is ready, the focus of the programme has shifted to making the public aware of its availability. This will be a large-scale publicity campaign, with AdOne delivering the television advertisements. Other suppliers and other teams within

High Tech will be delivering the projects related to print and web advertising.

Communication requirements of projects versus programmes

One difference between project and programme communication is that much higher levels of information shape programme communication. In a project, the inputs to project communication relate to the needs of the (usually well-defined) user group, and the progress that is made on the project; but in a programme, information about the interdependencies and progress of all the projects and implementation activities is also included. However, even though the following section focuses on the project team's communication efforts, the principles could easily be applied to the programme team.

3.1 GETTING STARTED – STARTING THE PROJECT

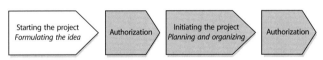

Key messages to communicate
- The benefits of the project and its contribution to the strategic direction of the organization
- The criteria by which the project will be judged a success
- How the project will be run.

Audience
- Sponsor
- Senior user
- Project and programme managers.

A project is triggered by a mandate from senior management, outlining the idea for the project and indicating any constraints within which it must be delivered, such as a deadline or expected budget. Additional information about the possible project will be developed, including identification of the business benefits that the project will deliver and the contribution that the project will make to the organization's strategy. Decisions will need to be taken about how the project will probably be delivered, including the staff who will be involved, whom they will report to and where they will be based. The Project Brief will be created as a formal record of this information, and it forms the basis of any announcements about the project.

Communication in the early stages – building rapport

It is important that the sponsor and the project manager are identified as early as possible in this process, as they are the two key players who will direct and undertake this early work. A relationship will need to be established between them, as the project manager will need the support and commitment of the sponsor throughout the life of the project. In addition, the sponsor will provide advice and take decisions about the different options presented by the project manager. Although the sponsor is probably more senior in the organization than the project manager, the project manager is more likely to take responsibility for building this rapport.

The project manager can develop rapport by setting up one or more meetings to discuss the values and objectives that will underpin the project. The sponsor has overall responsibility and accountability for the project within the organization, and will have opinions about how the work should be conducted, and what aspects of the project are the most important to get right. The project manager needs to discover what these ideas are, and provide reassurance through evidence of past experience that he or she shares the values of the sponsor and will deliver the project according to them.

In a programme, the programme manager will develop each Project Brief and use this as the first formal communication with each project manager. The programme manager understands that the success of the programme is dependent on the success of every project within the programme, and therefore they are likely to take a proactive stance to ensure that the project managers are given management support and commitment. This might include addressing a project manager's line manager, as well as introducing each project manager to their peers within the programme and to members of the programme office and the relevant business change managers, thus encouraging a supportive environment from the beginning.

In a programme environment, the programme manager may take the lead in building the rapport with the programme sponsor and other senior managers who are committed to the delivery of the programme.

Case study: establishing communication in the new project at AdOne

Establishing communication with the sponsor: This campaign is important for AdOne, and the sponsorship of the CEO makes it high profile. The project manager needs to get together with the CEO to discuss priorities for the project, and thereby identify the criteria by which the project will be judged a success. To do this, the project manager must arrange a suitable amount of time with the CEO, when there will be no interruptions. An early morning session, before the distractions of the day kick in, might be helpful. This also means there is less chance that the session will be postponed due to other meetings running late. The project manager could even suggest a 'neutral' venue so that they can meet as equals, one professional to another, rather than as boss and subordinate.

The sponsor is responsible for identifying the links between the project and the strategy for the organization, and must ensure that this is communicated to the project manager. This is because it is a valuable input to the creation of the Business Case, which summarizes the justification for the project. For example, in AdOne, the CEO knows that the company's strategy is to be seen as a high-quality, reliable provider of exciting campaigns. Therefore, the creation of a quality product is essential. The CEO must make it clear to the project manager that cutting corners and sloppy work would result in the worst possible outcome for AdOne, so there must be tight control of the suppliers. She also points out that High-Tech must love the campaign, so it will be essential to keep close to their requirements as the ideas take shape.

Establishing communication with the senior user:
At this early stage of the project, the project manager must develop a good understanding of the priorities of the senior user and the expectations that they have for how the project is to be run. For example, the senior user may have strong views on the amount of user involvement throughout the life of the project or how much authority they are willing to delegate to their staff to agree completion of project deliverables. There may be a set of 'unwritten rules' that the senior user does not feel obliged to articulate because 'all of my staff know how I work'. This is not of much help to the project manager or members of the project team who may unwittingly break the rules, e.g. by scheduling the involvement of users in focus groups or review panels that the senior user does not consider appropriate. It is easy for bad feeling to develop between the senior user and the project team, but this can be avoided if there is a clear understanding from the beginning on both sides about the expectations and ways of working.

As with the meeting between the project manager and sponsor, the project manager should arrange time with the senior user, probably as a one-to-one meeting. As part of this communication, the project manager will need to show empathy for the situation facing the senior user. In many organizations, the senior user is an experienced operational manager who has business-as-usual responsibilities as well as being the senior user on multiple projects. They may have a high degree of frustration with the project work as it takes them away from their day job, or they may be frustrated because what they ask for is not always delivered by the projects. In these situations, it is advisable for the project manager to allow the senior user to vent their feelings and describe the difficulties they are facing before telling them how the project manager intends to run this project.

The director of market research at AdOne is responsible for articulating the requirement of the buying public for the High-Tech software. However, at the same time the director will also be running a number of other research projects, possibly sponsoring them and advising other campaigns within AdOne. He will be looking for reassurance from the project manager that the project team will listen to the research, and respect the answers it is providing for the questions posed by the project. The project manager will need to explain to him how the project team will work, possibly outlining how the project team will be building a relationship with staff at High-Tech – not to contradict the results of the research but to enhance the project team's understanding of it.

3.2 GETTING STARTED – AUTHORIZATION

Key messages to communicate
- The work carried out during start up has been accepted
- There is commitment by senior management to start the initiation of the project.

Audience
- Project and programme managers
- Any members of the project team who are in place at this point in time
- All those impacted by the project or programme.

At the end of formulating an idea, the senior management must decide if the project is worthwhile and viable. If this is agreed, authorization is given at this point to commit resources to initiation. A communication should take place to notify all those likely to be impacted by the project and prepare them in case their involvement is needed. It might be decided to keep this low key until after initiation, when more information will be available.

Before sending out any communication, clarify the desired outcome of the announcement, and plan the information that will be communicated to achieve it.

Positive announcements

At this point in the project lifecycle, the most likely outcome is a call to action, asking staff to take part in requirements gathering, or being prepared to show members of the project team how work is currently carried out, so that they can appreciate what will need to be created by the project to improve the situation. Therefore, the tone of the message will need to be positive and it should emphasize the anticipated benefits of the project.

If the announcement is going out to all staff, it is not possible to tune the contents of the communication to meet the needs of any one particular communication preference. Therefore, the communication will need to address as many preferences as possible. Figure 3.4 shows how different parts of the overall message can be crafted to meet the needs of different preferences.

Negative announcements

If the effort is potentially contentious in nature, such as a reorganization or merger situation, senior managers may wish to hold several question and answer sessions with large groups of users to explain the justification for the initiative and alleviate fears. In this case, the sender of the communication is important. The seriousness of the communication needs to be matched by the seniority of the sender. If a junior manager is asked to inform staff about potential job losses, those affected may assume that the company does not take the situation seriously, or that the senior managers do not care about the impact of the project on the staff. In these situations, it should be recognised that not all outcomes can necessarily be achieved through one single announcement, and the outcome of each communication must be planned.

For example, when there are to be job losses at the end of a project, it is not in the interests of the company that staff become so distracted by this threat that their immediate productivity falls, or for talented staff to start looking for new jobs. In this case, it may be better to emphasize the efficiency benefits that the project will bring, rather than addressing the potential for job losses; or if job losses are to be mentioned, further communications must be planned that will explain in detail the criteria on which these will be based.

Figure 3.4 Announcing the project

AD   Announcement

Positive, upbeat message

For those who prefer the bigger picture

We are delighted to announce that AdOne has been chosen to produce an exciting new campaign for high-tech software.

This fits with the AdOne strategy for growing the business. There are plans to use this campaign as a showcase for larger telecoms and IT company accounts, so there are likely to be further business benefits once the project is completed.

For those who prefer sameness

For those who prefer difference

There are similarities between the proposed campaign and our award-winning campaign for Panther soft drinks, so we need to keep up the good work.

This campaign will be our first for a software supplier, so there will be lots of new product information to learn.

For those who prefer options

Access to plan is given for those who prefer details, but plan is not included so it does not put off those who prefer the bigger picture

Work on the Project Plan is about to commence and will be available on the intranet. Ideas for casting agencies, location scouts and storyboards will be warmly welcomed.

The project will be run using our 'AdOne for success' project framework (see http://projectsuccess for details).

For those who prefer procedures

3.3 GETTING STARTED – INITIATING AND DEFINING THE PROJECT, PLANNING AND ORGANIZING THE WORK

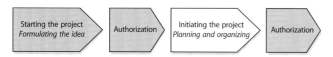

Key messages to communicate
- There is a realistic plan to manage this project, and the project can be delivered within the time and cost constraints that have been set for it
- We are all professionals and we are happy to work together on this project.

Audience
- Members of the project teams
- Staff who will be impacted by the project or programme.

Establishing relationships

During the development of the plan, a great deal of information will be exchanged between different teams, inside and outside the project. Time and cost estimates need to be established and requirements need to be gathered. This is a challenging time, especially on larger projects where there is often pressure from senior management to 'stop planning and just get on with it'. The process of initiation runs more effectively if there are strong relationships between the participants and trust in the answers being provided. Development of meaningful rapport between participants is often based on respect for each other's abilities and past experience. Therefore, it is important that before the teams begin working together, steps are taken to enable them to establish this mutual respect.

One of the easiest ways to achieve this is by asking each team to present to the others a summary of the work they will be doing and how they will be doing it. While using this as the framework of the communication, mention can be made about the qualifications of the team members, their past experience, and the similarities to past successes. This establishes each team and its members as 'professional and knowledgeable', and sets a baseline on which future relationships can be formed.

Real world experience
'The team at X Limited were always late on conference calls and it used to drive my staff crazy. We thought it was disrespectful because we ended up wasting a lot of our time waiting for them. We started turning up late because they were always late and the problems were spiralling out of control. Things got a lot better when we went to visit them at X's building. We saw how busy the rooms were and if the previous meeting was overrunning, they could not get into the room on time. Once we saw their problems, it was easier to appreciate that sometimes they were late, but to be fair to them, they also started making more of an effort to be on time.'

Case study: implications for AdOne and High-Tech

AdOne is a creative agency, and the design team is fairly new to the job. The team members have not worked for a software client before. The team from High-Tech knows the product and how it works, but this team has not briefed a creative agency before. Therefore, the first step is to bring the two teams together, so that they can get to know each other, and if possible develop a common language and set of terms before the requirements gathering begins. Otherwise, there will be many opportunities for misunderstandings, and the design team may misrepresent the product in the advertisements. To break down barriers further, the teams should visit each other's offices, so that each can gain an appreciation of the other organization as a whole. It is always easier to appreciate someone else's situation if you can picture where they work.

A similar approach is helpful in a programme environment, especially where there are several interdependencies between the projects and the need to share information is essential. For example, in High-Tech, the project teams working on the different advertising campaigns would benefit from close and trusting working relationships that would allow them to share information about the intended audience for their campaigns and the key message for each campaign. This might increase the consistency and overall quality of the advertising aspects of the programme.

Other communication techniques

There are a number of formal communication techniques that can increase the effectiveness of the initiation stage by making it easy to share information and keep everyone informed of what has been decided and what needs to be worked on next. For example, holding frequent, but short, team meetings will assist with the relationship building between team members and ensure that no-one is getting left behind in the exchange of information. Project support can organize many of these events and help the information sharing process. Creation of a team blog, team calendars, agendas, minutes and email reminders for meetings is important during initiation and once the project has been authorized and the work commences. If a discussion board for stakeholders is not in place already, it may be created at this point in order to capture feedback from the stakeholder groups to ensure they have a voice in the planning process and will give it their support. If stakeholders feel ignored or shut out of the process, they may impede progress. See Appendix A for more details about communication techniques.

The Communications Plan

Throughout the life of the project or programme, communication activities will require time and effort that is not always fully reflected in the activities scheduled on the Project Plan or Programme Plan. Therefore, it is helpful to establish a Communications Plan that sets out all of these activities and assigns resources to them.

The scope of the plan covers regular communications. There will be a need for ad hoc communication throughout the project or programme lifecycle in response to different events, but as these are unexpected they will not form part of the plan. The plan should state what messages are to be sent to which stakeholders, when this is to be done and by whom. Activities for gathering feedback from stakeholders should also be included in the plan.

In a programme environment, each of the projects will be responsible for communicating to their own stakeholders. However, it is important that the programme manager coordinates this effort, to ensure that the messages from each project are consistent with the scope and objectives of the programme, and that information from one project does not conflict with or contradict information from another project or the programme itself. Therefore, it might be helpful for the programme manager to define the strategy or approach for all programme communications. This should cover:

- What the key messages are for the programme as a whole, so that any project communications can include this information or refer to it
- Identification of who within the programme and within individual projects are responsible for the different communication roles. For example, for certain stakeholders it might be appropriate that the same person is always responsible for the communication, or certain types of message always communicated by the programme sponsor or manager
- How stakeholders are to be grouped and categorized
- Who is responsible for each group of stakeholders: those stakeholders who are impacted by only one project; those stakeholders who are impacted by more than one project; and those stakeholders who are the responsibility of the programme overall

- How interfaces between the programme and the stakeholders will be managed
- How feedback and dialogue with the stakeholders will be referred to by each of the projects so that there is a two-way flow of information within the programme itself and from the programme and its projects to the 'outside world'.

3.4 GETTING STARTED – AUTHORIZATION

> **Key messages to communicate**
> - The work carried out in the initiation stage has been accepted
> - There is commitment by senior management to resource the work outlined in the Project Plan
> - Supplier relationships can now commence.
>
> **Audience**
> - Project and programme managers and project teams
> - All those impacted by the project or programme
> - Suppliers and those not chosen as suppliers.

For the majority of projects, senior management will require a formal meeting and presentation by the project manager prior to authorizing the start of any specialist work on the project. Although the sponsor is responsible and accountable overall for the project, the project manager also has a vested interest in the project being authorized. At the very least, the project manager wants their work during the initiation stage to be validated. In addition, without a project, the project manager may not have a role within the organization.

The project manager should take time to plan the outcome of the authorization meeting and identify each of the messages that need to be included. Figure 3.5 shows five outcomes that a project or programme manager should identify as integral to achieving authorization.

In a programme environment, the programme manager will present documentation that defines all aspects of the programme – benefits to be achieved, the required projects and a blueprint of the organization once the programme has been completed.

The authorization meeting

For those who have a visual preference, the 'professionalism' of any presentation or handouts will be important, as any discrepancies that this type of preference 'sees' can act as a block to what they hear. For example, even the logo of the organization appearing in the wrong colour on the presentation can 'interfere' with the message being given. The same applies to spelling errors or formatting errors such as text not lining up in a graphic.

Those with an auditory preference will be easily distracted by noise. Therefore, ensure that the room chosen for the presentation is quiet, and make sure all participants turn off their phones. Put up a 'Do Not Disturb' notice on the door. Speak clearly, and try to ensure that the presentation flows with very few 'ums and ahs' and 'I don't knows'. If any team member is not a confident speaker, they should rehearse their talk beforehand.

People with a kinaesthetic preference will be impacted by the environment in which they attend the presentation. For example, this group will often notice the temperature of the room or the layout of the seats. Thoughtful gestures such as the provision of water and notepads and pens will help this group to engage with the presentation. The kinaesthetic preference enjoys demonstrations and experiences so some engagement with the subject being presented should be included. For example, senior managers can be supplied with a copy of the Project Plan, and take part in an exercise to identify the key review points for the rest of the project.

Communicating the authorization

Once the decision has been taken to go ahead with the project, this information will need to be communicated to any supplier organizations that will be involved. There may also be a requirement to notify any suppliers that tendered for business but were not successful – that their services are not required this time. Each of these communications can be created specifically for the intended audience, so consideration should be given to the outcome that is required.

Figure 3.5 Authorization agenda

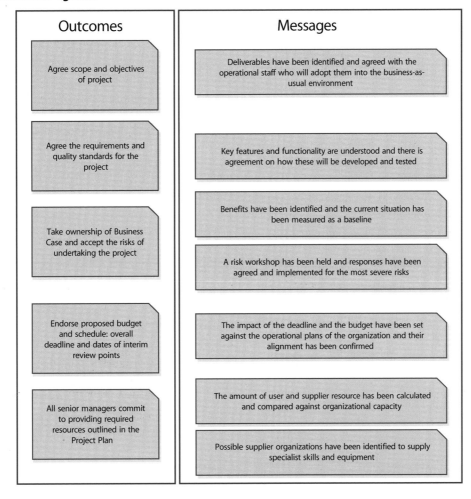

Outcomes	Messages
Agree scope and objectives of project	Deliverables have been identified and agreed with the operational staff who will adopt them into the business-as-usual environment
Agree the requirements and quality standards for the project	Key features and functionality are understood and there is agreement on how these will be developed and tested
Take ownership of Business Case and accept the risks of undertaking the project	Benefits have been identified and the current situation has been measured as a baseline
	A risk workshop has been held and responses have been agreed and implemented for the most severe risks
Endorse proposed budget and schedule: overall deadline and dates of interim review points	The impact of the deadline and the budget have been set against the operational plans of the organization and their alignment has been confirmed
All senior managers commit to providing required resources outlined in the Project Plan	The amount of user and supplier resource has been calculated and compared against organizational capacity
	Possible supplier organizations have been identified to supply specialist skills and equipment

Communicating positive outcomes

For those suppliers that have been selected to work on the project or programme, the desired outcomes of this message are:

- They have the right skills for the job
- The organization is looking forward to working with them on this project
- The supplier must prioritize this project above other work for any other clients.

As with the meeting to discover values that took place between the sponsor and the project manager, it is a good idea for the project manager to undertake a similar exercise with the suppliers.

Case study: implications for AdOne

TeleFilm has worked with AdOne before, but the project manager has not worked with the TeleFilm team manager. Without a past relationship to call on, both parties do not know what the other is looking for so there is no quick way that can make negotiations about schedules and budgets between them easier. The project manager could offer to visit the team manager for TeleFilm at its premises. This would also have the advantage that the project manager could experience the atmosphere of TeleFilm and gain a wider understanding of the company overall and not just the perspective of the team manager. It is useful to decide an agenda ahead of this meeting, so that both parties can agree the purpose (even though the main aims of the session is to create rapport and hopefully the sharing of less work-related and more personal information).

Real world experience

'Winning the contract is just the beginning and it would be great if we can hold some kind of social event before the work starts just to get to know each other. I want to be respected for my work, but it's also a lot easier if I am liked, so going out for a sandwich or inviting the project manager round for a tour of our offices can work wonders.'

Communicating negative outcomes

For those suppliers that have not been selected, it is important to ensure that the outcome does not create problems with the relationship between the two organizations. Just because a company was not selected this time does not mean that it might not be the right supplier for other projects. Ideally, the communication would be in the form of a conversation so that the supplier is able to check their understanding of the reasons why they were not successful and identify areas of improvement for future tender opportunities. However, this information must be sensitively delivered by the project or programme manager as there is a danger that the more reasons that are given why a supplier was not chosen could open up more avenues for that supplier to justify why they should have been chosen – which can become a lengthy circular argument.

3.5   MAKING PROGRESS – DAY-TO-DAY CONTROL

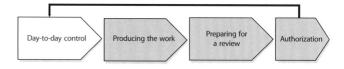

Key messages to communicate
- Establishing exactly what work will be done and within which constraints it will be delivered
- Telling project teams that they need to deliver more work for less time or money.

Audience
- Project and programme managers
- Project teams.

Once the project has been authorized, effort is concentrated on getting the work under way, identifying the progress that is being made and handling issues and problems that arise.

Communicating by email versus meeting

In a project, the project manager is responsible for authorizing each piece of work listed on the Project Plan to the relevant team manager. In a programme, the programme manager briefs each project manager on the scope, objectives, timeframe, budget and quality requirements for their project. If this information is communicated formally via email, it can serve as a useful confirmation of what was originally asked for as work progresses.

For example, a project manager can set out their requirements for the work that a particular team manager has to undertake. However, if this is the only communication between the team manager and the project manager before work commences there is a high likelihood of the requirements being misunderstood and misinterpreted. Therefore, the project manager and team manager should meet to review key elements of the work. A meeting gives both parties the opportunity to give immediate feedback on what they each think, and this will speed up the process far more than a lengthy exchange of emails.

> **Real world experience**
>
> 'When we are getting things started, I always schedule twice as much time with the team as I think I will need – and we usually use it.'
>
> 'It is now routine for me to ask the team manager to document the results of our "kick off" meeting. That way, I can immediately see if there is any confusion between what I thought we had agreed and what he thinks.'

A regular communication that the project manager will have with the project teams is about getting more for less. As the project moves forward, planning assumptions and estimates may prove to be optimistic and things take longer to complete, or cost more to do than was originally

scheduled or budgeted for. The effect is that the project manager has to try to reduce the time or cost of other activities to make up for this.

The method and approach used by the project manager in these situations can make the difference between success and failure. For example, the probable reactions to the email in Figure 3.6 may not be helpful.

Figure 3.6 Example of an unhelpful email

```
To: samir.khan@adone.com; john.nichols@adone.com; jamie.spear@adone.com
From: susan.williams@adone.com

Dear all
As you know, time is tight on this project, and we are only three months
away from the deadline. Over running will not be tolerated, so please
do not allow any of your activities to run late, even by a day.
If anyone is off sick, can you please ensure that they make up the
time at the weekends.

Regards,
Susan
```

The general nature of the email in Figure 3.6 will make each team manager feel that their own special circumstances have not been taken into account, so they will either be offended, or simply not feel that the email is really meant for them. Team managers whose activities are running on time may feel they are being criticized for something that they have not done. By addressing this email to everyone, the project manager is creating distance between themselves and the team managers. Using negative language such as 'Do not allow' can cause the receiver of the message unnecessary confusion, because this phrase prompts the question 'So what am I allowed to do?'. The action required by the project manager is not as clear as it appears in the email.

A more helpful approach would be for the project manager to have one-to-one meetings with each of the team managers, and go over their part of the schedule in detail, understanding all of the activities that they have planned. This is a chance for the project manager to explain how any delays will affect the ultimate project deadline, and ask each team manager to help in ensuring that this does not happen. It also gives the team managers an opportunity to have their say, after which they are ready to hear the message from the project manager.

Case study: time for a meeting

The AdOne project manager may be particularly worried about possible delays from the editing team, as this is a resource that is shared across the company. The project manager has to ensure that the work for the High-Tech project is treated as a priority and does not get rescheduled in favour of other company initiatives. A general email such as the one above would have a negative impact on the morale and attitudes of the members of the editing team, and could destroy any rapport that the project manager has established with them.

A meeting to discuss scheduling issues, where both parties can come to the table with their concerns and there can be a real exchange of information, should clarify any misunderstandings. If there is pressure from other parts of AdOne on the editing team, the project manager can take responsibility for addressing these, and remove the team manager from being caught between two bosses.

3.6 MAKING PROGRESS – PRODUCING THE WORK

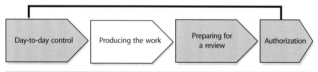

Day-to-day control → Producing the work → Preparing for a review → Authorization

Key messages to communicate
- Progress information from the project teams
- Early warning of issues, risks and problems that have the capacity to impede the progress of the project.

Audience
- Project and programme managers
- Project teams
- Sponsor
- Senior user
- Senior supplier.

Streamlining communication

There may be many streams of work happening at the same time, so it is important that regular and reliable progress information is being captured. This can be in the form of a formal report, an email or oral exchange. Whichever method is used, the information must include:

- Progress to date
- What is left to do
- Issues that have been encountered and how they have been overcome
- Risks that could impact on any future work.

The project manager should establish a fixed structure to the frequency and format of the reporting from each of the team managers. This ensures that although the information exchanged each time will be different, the mechanism remains the same. Comparing like with like makes it easier to identify the changes in content, i.e. the progress that has been made. It is much harder to understand the progress that has been made if the format in which this is communicated is different every time. However, the usefulness of the reports can vary. The most effective reports are those that address the communication preferences of the project manager, as this makes them instinctively feel as if the team manager is 'on their wavelength'. This also has an effect on the amount of trust that the project manager has in the team manager.

Case study: communication in the programme environment

The programme manager has to establish a structure for communication between themselves and the project managers. This can also be extended to include a regular information exchange between the programme manager and the business change manager(s) so that the flow of information within the programme includes project information and the preparation activities and level of readiness within impacted operational departments.

Within High-Tech, the programme manager will meet with the project managers responsible for the television, print and web advertising projects, but will also meet with the communications director to ensure the communications department within High-Tech is ready to implement the campaigns and integrate them into all of the other promotional activities that High-Tech undertakes.

In a programme, the programme manager and business change manager are on a par with each other so the business change manager does not have an obligation to formally report directly to the programme manager and the programme manager does not have to report directly to the business change manager. Therefore, this communication will rely heavily on the rapport that is established between the two, and the level of trust that they each have in the other's ability.

> **Real world experience**
>
> 'As soon as I hear the words "new direction" and "different approach" I start to get worried. I think the best approach to project management is to do what we have done before. Being told how we have invented new ways of doing the same thing leads me to conclude that the project team have too much time on their hands.'
>
> 'I like to hear about the details, and a couple of lines telling me that everything is going according to plan immediately makes me suspicious. I want proof, and if I don't get it, I will go looking for it.'
>
> 'One of my direct reports always uses capitals in his mails to me. In my view, he is shouting at me, and it really winds me up. Whenever I read anything he has written, I am always in a bad mood.'

Case study: addressing communication preferences

The team manager from TeleFilm has a standard way of communicating progress on any filming project. He is happy to chat with the project manager and during the conversation he will give full disclosure of any problems or issues, how they are being handled and what the effect is on the work. He speaks very quickly, with great passion for his work, highlighting the different options that are available for the next steps and why each of them might work. However, the project manager for AdOne is a very disciplined person, and prefers to receive her information in written form and in sequential order, rather than letting a conversation cover lots of different directions. She prefers a step-by-step approach to the way forward, and likes to hear the lower-level detail. She firmly believes that writing a progress report is an important discipline, because it is only when things are written down that the issues become clear and the way forward can be identified.

Clearly, these two managers have a very different approach to communication. Even though the team manager from TeleFilm is doing a great job, the project manager is unhappy with the progress, as she has no written reports as evidence. The more concerned the project manager becomes, the more questions she has for the team manager, who is starting to feel that he is on the phone to her every minute. His frustration is growing, so he gives less detail in each conversation, exacerbating the problem.

To break this vicious circle, the two managers need to take time out to discover their value systems, and understand each other's communication preferences. Once this has been done, they can reach a compromise about how to communicate in the future.

> **Real world experience**
>
> 'I hate these touchy feely meetings, but I have learnt over the years that any breakdown in communications is clouding the real issue of whether the project is running OK or not. Getting the team out for a drink and telling them that I just need the written reports to keep Audit happy can go a long way to getting things back on track. They start to see me as the guy under pressure from Audit, rather than the guy who just wants to count the paperclips whilst they get on with the real work.'

Information escalation processes

Although the progress information is communicated directly to the project manager in the first instance, there may be occasions when this information has to be escalated to senior management (sponsor, senior user and senior supplier). The project manager will need to agree how this escalation process should work and the format and contents of the communications that take place during this process.

To ensure an effective escalation process, the project manager should identify the preferred communication method for each manager. For example, the senior supplier might be out of the office most of the time, relying on their Blackberry™ to keep in touch. Therefore, short messages without large attachments are most appropriate for them.

When escalating 'bad' news, the language used can have a significant effect on the message received. For example, if the message header is 'Important' or 'Urgent', the sender must be aware of the emotion that the receiver will attach to these words. 'Urgent' to some recipients may mean 'stop everything else and only concentrate on this', which is fine if that is what is needed, but if the project manager used the word urgent to mean 'this will have significant impact on the relationship with supplier X, so I need you to advise me what I should say to them when we meet tomorrow', the mismatch in interpretation of words will cause annoyance to the receiver.

A simple way to overcome some of these difficulties is to 'match' the language that senior managers use in the communications that they send out, as this is a good indication of their interpretation of these emotive terms.

3.7 MAKING PROGRESS – PREPARING FOR A REVIEW

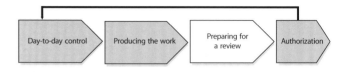

Key messages to communicate
- Accuracy of completed work
- Detailed plans for upcoming work
- Sound reasoning for continuing work.

Audience
- Audit or assurance function.

When preparing for an official review, the primary message to convey is one of confidence that the work planned for in the current stage has actually been completed and that the results are fit for purpose. In order for the decision-makers to commit the appropriate amount of resources and budget, they need to see and authorize a detailed plan of the work for the next stage.

The project documentation should represent an honest and objective picture of this information, and the project manager should also prepare a summary of how the objectives of the project relate to the current business environment, so that the decision-makers can assess if the effort remains worthwhile and viable.

As part of preparing for a review, there may be audit or assurance functions that need to be satisfied that the project is delivering according to schedule, budget and quality expectations, and that it is being managed according to the standards and methods expected by the organization.

The project manager will be primarily responsible for communicating with these functions, and should take time to discover the communication preferences of the receiver (Figure 3.7). The desired outcome of any audit or assurance communication is to provide sufficient data to reassure and convince those who are overseeing the project that all is well. For example, by the very nature of the role, the auditor may have a preference for hearing about the problems associated with the project rather than a more positive and upbeat message about the progress that is being made. This might be accompanied by a preference for details rather than the bigger picture, including step-by-step guides for how any problems are being tackled, rather than a more general set of options about how things might be fixed.

Figure 3.7 Audit announcement

AD 'Next Biggest Thing' project review

> For those who prefer external validation

The designs for each of the six adverts within the campaign have been ratified against the requirements provided by High-Tech staff and confirmation has been received from the senior user that these requirements are in line with the results from the market research.

> Detailed, factual message that is tailored for the audience of auditors

All of the High-Tech team attended the meeting, which was chaired by Dan Roberts, head of the design team. The message, format, structure and content of each advert were presented and compared against the expected demographics of the target audience.

> For those who prefer external validation

> Access to guidelines is provided for those who prefer procedures and details focus, but these are not included so it does not distract those who prefer the bigger picture

A number of additional points and amendments were discussed and changes to the designs were agreed as part of the meeting. These amendments have been documented and can be accessed at http://Des16Cam5Advert1.

The requirements have been gathered according to the 'AdOne for success' project framework (see http://projectsuccess for details) and the designs have been created according to the design guidelines agreed company-wide for television advertising (http://desguide2008).

> For those who prefer sameness and procedures

> For those who prefer difference

As this is the first set of designs for a software supplier, a number of advisers were consulted and a referral was made to MediaWatch and Accuracy in Media for their guidelines on the subject. Their publicatons are available from the project office.

> For those who prefer external validation

Market research has held three focus groups since the requirements received sign off, and the feedback has been very positive.

Case study: communicating with the audit function

At the end of the design stage of the High-Tech commercials, a series of meetings have taken place to check that the designs and the requirements given by High-Tech have been met. Senior management at AdOne will not want to give the go-ahead for filming in the absence of this reassurance. Therefore, the details of these meetings need to be communicated to the audit or assurance function.

3.8   MAKING PROGRESS – AUTHORIZATION

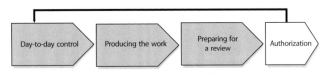

Key messages to communicate
- Continuation or termination
- Celebrate successes.

Audience
- Project or programme managers
- Project team
- All those who have contributed to the project so far or who are impacted by the project.

The decision taken at this point either allows for the work to continue on to the next stage or tranche, or requires it to close down in a controlled manner. Regardless of the outcome of this decision, successes and achievements should be celebrated.

The announcement

When the decision-makers agree to authorize the next stage, this decision and the achievements to date should be acknowledged and the team's efforts formally recognized.

If the decision-makers wish to close the effort down prematurely on the basis of the evidence presented, the team's efforts to date should still be recognized. The reasons for closing down prematurely can vary enormously. Just because a project is closing down does not mean the team did not do everything right. If the initiative no longer makes sense in the current environment, it is the responsibility of the decision-makers to close it down. However, the team's efforts should not be overshadowed by this.

In programme terms, completion of a tranche indicates a step change in capability has been achieved. Whilst the whole intended transformation has not yet been achieved, it may be decided that the programme has achieved many of its benefits at this point, and full transformation is no longer required.

Preparing for the authorization meeting

It is important for the project manager to establish the context for the authorization meeting. The project manager is living and breathing the project every day, but that is not true for the senior managers. Therefore, the project manager will need to communicate information on 'How we got to this point' before presenting the decision-makers with any requests for authorization. This is also true for a programme manager, who will have comprehensive knowledge of the progress of all of the projects that have run during the tranche.

An effective way of summarizing how we got to this point is to offer decision-makers a visual presentation of the timeline, rather than asking them to read reams of information. A poster or model can be produced as part of a slide presentation and will help those with a kinaesthetic preference as they can stand up and examine the timeline and fully engage with it.

As part of the process of authorization, it is essential that the senior managers feel sufficiently well informed about the project to be able to make a decision. They rely on the communications they receive from the project manager and any audit or assurance function that they have appointed to the project.

The project or programme manager may have to present to the senior managers, which means that establishing rapport with them will be useful, as it will enable the presentation to be 'tuned' to meet their values and priorities, as well as addressing their communication preferences.

Case study: meeting communication preferences

To reassure senior management that problems are not being ignored, AdOne's 'Next Biggest Thing' project manager begins her presentation with an outline of each of the difficulties experienced in the stage. To satisfy those preferring a positive communication, she gives examples of how each of those problems was overcome or how, by encountering the problem at this point in the lifecycle, further information has been uncovered, which will help the overall delivery of the project.

The project manager provides a presentation pack to those with a kinaesthetic preference, so they have an actual product to take away from the presentation, whilst those of an auditory preference do not feel that they have to look at the slide presentation as they can review it at their leisure at a later point. For those who prefer to think over what they have heard before drawing a conclusion, an artificial break can be constructed, over coffee or lunch, where they can have some private time, before coming back to make a decision. An alternative way of providing this space is to have a question and answer session, where

they do not necessarily have to pose any questions but it does give them some valuable thinking time.

3.9 CLOSING DOWN – EVALUATION

> **Key messages to communicate**
> - Evaluation of what the project has achieved
> - Lessons learned.
>
> **Audience**
> - Project or programme managers
> - Project team
> - Sponsor
> - Senior user
> - Senior supplier
> - Everyone who has contributed to the project or programme.

At the end of the project, it is important to summarize the experiences and achievements of the team, setting them against the original objectives and plans. Any discrepancies between the plans and what was achieved will need to be explained, so that there is a record of why it happened and who agreed to it.

Analysing what went wrong and what went well

There is an opportunity for the organization to learn from each project experience, and improve the capability for delivering successful projects. Lessons usually tend to focus on what could be learned from the things that went badly and alternatives or suggestions can be made for doing things differently. However, it is equally important to recognize what went well during the effort and provide recommendations for ways to repeat these.

Information can be gathered throughout the project lifecycle, but it is only when all work has been completed that a period of evaluation can take place. The project manager will be responsible for the information gathering and the initial reporting to senior management, and an agreement will need to be made with senior management about the ownership of any follow-up activities that are identified.

Internal and external feedback

Communication at this point in the project is directed at getting feedback rather than sending out broadcast messages. Feedback should be collected from everyone who has been involved or impacted by the project. If those who have been negatively impacted by the project are not given an opportunity to air their views, handover and adoption of the projects' outputs may be slower than expected.

Once the suppliers have completed their contracts, there is a chance that the information that they have gained from working on the project will be lost, so it is helpful to get their impressions of what should be done differently next time. It is unlikely that any supplier would volunteer a formal summary of lessons learned for fear of impacting their chances of working with the organization again. Therefore, the project manager will need to ensure that this is kept informal and may even need to promise that the information will be reported back in a non-attributed manner, so that the source remains confidential.

Real world experience

'Once all the work was done, just listening to what the suppliers thought about how we organized things was really enlightening. They thought we came across as really professional because we were so organized at the start of the project, and they said that made them make a lot more effort in answering our questions promptly and getting us the information that we needed.'

'Although the suppliers were impressed about how much we knew about our product range, they pointed out that we tended to use a lot of jargon and acronyms which they didn't know. They felt they were always asking us to explain ourselves, which took time and could be very annoying. Until they told us, I had no idea, but once the meeting was over, I started to notice that we really do speak in code sometimes so we are trying to stop this now.'

Role of communication in gathering information

Before planning any information gathering communication, the project manager will need to give careful thought to the atmosphere/environment that exists across the project teams and supplier resources. If significant problems and failures have been experienced on the project, a great deal of blame may have been communicated between the participants. So the project manager could consider that this might be an opportunity to rebuild relationships and close the project on a positive note. The success of this will depend on the ability of the project manager to tune their communications to the specific preferences of those involved, and the strength of the rapport that has been built between the project manager and these resources.

Case study: communicating appropriately during closure

AdOne's project manager wishes to address members of the TeleFilm team who have been identified as very visual and kinaesthetic, and who like the big picture and draw their validation from external sources. Her communication must include the following factors:

- An informal setting with no formal barriers to getting close to people – therefore, a social setting with an opportunity to shake hands and thank people face to face.

- A thank-you speech that includes reference to how much the efforts of the team have contributed to a great campaign, including viewing figures or customer comments about how innovative or creative the adverts are. Thank-you speeches can be enhanced to include 'mini' award ceremonies, where individual members of the team are identified as the 'best of something'. This can be light-hearted and relate to the banter that has built up on the team during the project, e.g. 'person who makes the best coffee', 'staff member most likely to break the printer', 'person who can get the most spelling mistakes into a progress report' etc.

Real world experience

'I think everyone likes to be recognized for the effort that they have put in, so we always do an awards ceremony at the end of the project. We get the sponsor to hand out the prizes, which are paid for from an entertainment kitty that everyone contributes to. Of course, if the project has gone well, the sponsor usually puts in extra money so the prizes are better, but otherwise it's just boxes of chocolates and things like that.'

Other communication approaches during closure

If the project manager is aware that members of the project team or other stakeholders have experienced problems during the project and they want to make sure that this is recorded, a more formal, one-to-one style of communication is appropriate. The project manager needs to arrange sufficient time and a quiet location, as this indicates that the session is being taken seriously and that the project manager is not just 'going through the motions'.

The project manager may need to establish a rapport with the participant before meaningful feedback can be given, so they may have to ask some general questions to get the conversation moving. Once a sense of trust has been established between the project manager and the participant, complaints can be heard and ideas for improving things in the future can be devised. If ideas are generated, it is important that the project manager acknowledges these by letting the participant know into which documentation they have been included and who is likely to read it.

Real world experience

'I dread asking for feedback, so I have to remind myself that it is an opportunity to hear what we did well alongside what went wrong.'

'It's amazing how some people bottle things up until the last minute, when there is no chance of them getting fixed. I try and ask for as much feedback as possible during the project, but there is still always a rush of new things to say at the end.'

For general points about how the project was run, a mass communication method such as a questionnaire can be useful. It is a good way of assessing whether stakeholders have felt included or well informed during the project and whether they perceived the project to have been well managed and organized. To ensure there is an opportunity for feedback, it should be made clear that those who wish to make specific points should contact the project manager directly.

3.10 CLOSING DOWN – HANDOVER

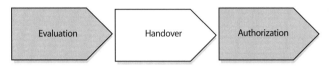

Key messages to communicate
- Customer acceptance of the products that have been created
- Handover documentation and demonstrations.

Audience
- Users who will adopt the new products and services that have been created by the project or programme.

Before the team can handover the deliverables to the operational units, they need to obtain formal acceptance that the products meet the requirements of the users. This is usually given by the senior user or can be delegated to a team nominated by the senior user. If all the products have been completed and tested, this step is more or less a formality. If the project has been closed prematurely, there is still the need to get acceptance for any products that have been created by the project and that are going to be used by the organization.

Once sign-off has been established, handover can commence. This ensures that the products created are understood by the operations and maintenance teams who will be responsible for them. The operational teams not only need the physical products created, but they also need the supporting documentation that accompanies them, such as the configuration management records.

This guarantees they receive a full understanding of how the products work and fit together. If the products cannot be used properly in operation, then they will not be able to produce the expected benefits in the future.

Communicating with operational units

The quality of the communications that are sent out by the project at this time may have an effect on how the products are viewed. If the communications about how products should be used are disorganized, incomplete or even inaccurate, there is a good chance that the users will think the same about the products themselves.

Case study: handover

AdOne can invite High-Tech staff to a special screening of the advertisements at a cinema. This creates a fun and 'off-duty' atmosphere and by treating the launch as a significant event, the project team is demonstrating that it is proud of its campaign, so High-Tech can be proud of it too.

Is the information clear?

The majority of the information that is created at this point is likely to come from the project teams and suppliers who have created the products. It is advisable, however, for them to be 'sense checked' before they are distributed. It is all too easy to use jargon, and assume a high base level of knowledge if you have been working on something from the very beginning. However, the users will not have these advantages and might therefore find the documents difficult to understand.

Real world experience
'Every time we get new user guides from the IT department, there is so much jargon I think only Bill Gates could understand it. The problem is, staff think that if the user guide is hard to read, the system is going to be impossible to use. It's not always true but it does put people off switching over to the new system.'

Usefulness of demonstrations

Demonstrations are an important method for generating a two-way flow of communication, so that users can ask questions directly and practise the new ways of working in a risk-free environment. To encourage feedback, an informal setting for demonstrations is helpful, as well as ensuring that the audience is a peer group rather than a hierarchical group of managers. Staff can feel inhibited about asking how something works when their manager is in the room.

The attitude of those giving the demonstration will affect the success of the event. The project manager must ensure that there is limited 'protection' of the products by their creators. In other words, if any member of the project team is sensitive to criticism, and reacts emotionally to it, consider if they are the right person to be demonstrating the product. Alternatively, ask a trainer or facilitator to run the session instead.

Alerting users about handover

A formal announcement that handover is about to take place can be helpful to alert users that they will soon be seeing and/or using the new products in operation. This early warning can help trigger management in the user groups to ensure that support and administration processes are in place if not done so already. A mass email might be the most useful to communicate this message to a wide range of users, and poster campaigns can generate awareness and interest and stimulate questions from staff to their managers.

Role of the business change manager

In a programme environment, handover of project deliverables triggers the transition activities planned by the business change manager. Therefore, many aspects of handover communication might be undertaken by them directly to their staff rather than involving the project team. This enables the business change manager to demonstrate ownership and commitment of the products and support for their implementation.

If the business change manager remains 'hands-off' during this process, it may be interpreted as a lack of support for the deliverables or a belief that the business change manager has had the project imposed upon them.

Case study: implications for the communications director

In High-Tech, full involvement of the communications director in announcing the delivery of the television advertisements from the AdOne project will create an atmosphere of excitement and anticipation within the communications department that will lead to the communications staff making time to see the advertisements, telling others about them and incorporating them into the other promotional activities that the department undertakes.

3.11 CLOSING DOWN – AUTHORIZATION

Key messages to communicate
- Official notification of closure
- Thank you messages.

Audience
- All staff who have contributed to or have been impacted by the project or programme.

There should be very little left to communicate at the end of the project. When the decision is taken to authorize the closure of the project, the sponsor and other senior managers may wish to send out an official notification. This confirms to the organization and all stakeholders that the work has ceased and that responsibility for the deliverables now rests within the operational units of the organization.

Case study: end of project – implications for future prospects

At AdOne, there may be some official closure activities that involve the CEO as the sponsor and her equivalent at High-Tech. In this case, there may be an opportunity to discuss the possibility of more business.

Acknowledging involvement

Any project is a tremendous effort, and project teams will appreciate acknowledgement of their efforts by senior management. Confirmation of project closure should also be sent to any other teams within the organization that have been impacted by the existence of the project. These might include the audit or assurance function, the procurement or contracts manager who managed the relationship with the suppliers, or the facilities manager who provided the space, furniture and facilities that were used by the project team.

Real world experience

'When a new project kicks off, everyone wants office space and meeting rooms. I am their best friend, they are on the phone all day chasing me. When they have finished, you would think I did not even exist. On one project, I didn't even know the space had been freed up until I did my usual weekly walk around the building. Facilities management keeps this organization running. Next time that project manager wants a meeting room, I am going to assign them to the nearest cupboard!'

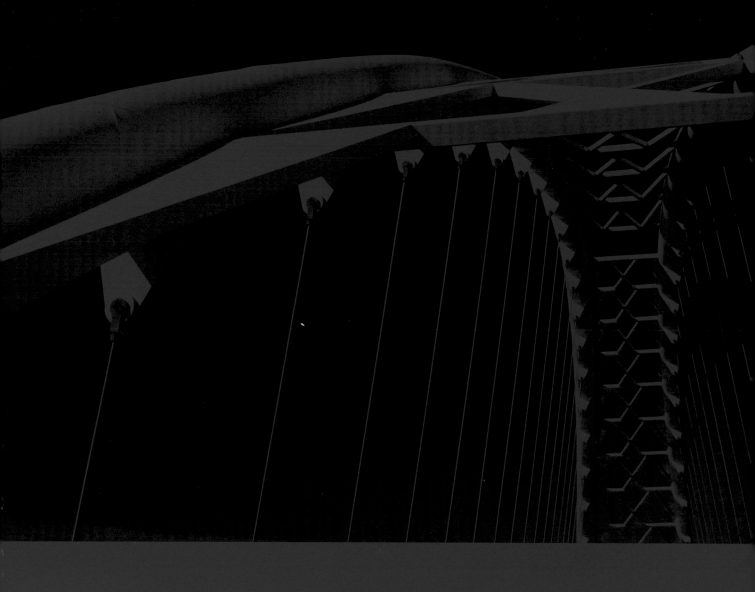

Appendices

Appendix A: Practical guide to effective communication

There is usually a great deal of information that needs to be communicated in a project or programme. However, consideration must always be given to how information can be shared, rather than simply presented, and how stakeholders can engage with the information and provide feedback.

The first consideration must be how specific each communication needs to be (Figure A.1). There are efficiency gains in sending out standard messages across all stakeholders, but this ignores the information needs of different stakeholder groups, and prevents any 'tailoring' of the message to address specific interests. The creation of individual messages to stakeholders can increase their buy-in and support to the project, but it is time consuming and runs the risk of creating different strata of stakeholders – those who are well informed and those who are on the periphery.

Figure A.1 Individual or multiple messages

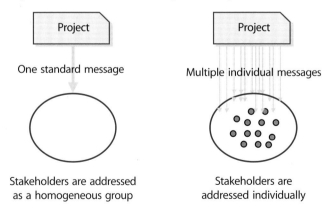

Another consideration in selecting the communication method is the level of demand and interest shown by

the stakeholder (Figure A.2). If the stakeholder is passive, then the most appropriate communication methods will not require any action on their part. However, active stakeholders can demand a great deal of project time, when the most efficient use of resources involves more passive forms of communication.

Figure A.2 Active and passive stakeholders

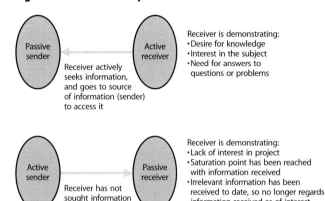

There are three main flows of project information:

- Presenting the message
- Working with stakeholders
- Receiving feedback on the message.

A.1 PRESENTING THE MESSAGE

A project can use a number of methods to push information out to the stakeholders:

- Email
- Newsletters
- Blogs

- Formal presentations
- Podcasts and vodcasts
- One-to-one meetings
- Question and answer sessions
- Poster campaigns.

A.2 CREATING EFFECTIVE PROJECT EMAILS

Surveys indicate that when an email is received, 11% of the recipients read it thoroughly, 57% skim-read it, 10% plan to read it (but do not get round to it), and 22% actively decide not to read it.

These figures can be improved by careful email design that takes into account a number of factors:

- Clarify the purpose of the email
- Clearly identify the audience
- Define the intended effect of the message
- Format the email to increase the read rate
- Clarify how the audience is expected to respond
- Ensure the message can be understood.

Clarify the purpose of the email

The first thing to decide is the purpose of the email. Is it a regular progress report, or does it announce a new initiative or a change that the reader will not have heard about via any other method of communication?

Next, consider what message the stakeholder should actually receive as a result of reading the email. For example, is the underlying message reassuring ('the project is making good progress so you don't have to worry') or is it a call to action ('the project is coming towards a significant date and effort is needed from users to take part in testing if the implementation date is to be met').

Another type of message is soliciting views from the stakeholders. However, this works well if one answer is being sought, but if there is a need to pose multiple

questions across a range of issues, it will probably be more effective and easier to collate the responses if a questionnaire or interview is used.

Clearly identify the audience

Make sure that the distribution list is relevant not only to the project overall, but for this particular message about the project. A golden rule is to always ask, 'What do I expect each recipient of this email to do with the information?'. If the answer is nothing, review why this stakeholder is being sent this information. Do not copy people into the email just because they have some connection to the project. Recipients will rapidly learn that the emails they receive are not relevant to them and are a version of email spam that they will ignore.

As well as sending the email only to those who need it, consider tailoring the content so that it is relevant for the different audiences in the distribution list. Emails are a very cheap form of communication, so the project team can afford to create different versions of the same email. This targeting can often be relatively simple – by, for example, prioritizing the information in the email differently so that the first paragraph addresses the specific concerns of that particular group. If one group of users is particularly concerned about the effect that a launch date will have on their day-to-day business, then this should be in the lead paragraph. Another group might be particularly concerned about whether the project is going to deliver a specific piece of functionality, so this should be in the lead paragraph in their email.

Define the intended effect of the message

If a significant change is being communicated, consider whether email is really the best way of doing it. One of the disadvantages of email communication is that it is regarded as a rather lazy and impersonal way of delivering important information. It is a great tool for communicating non-essential information such as progress information, as those it is sent to can store it and decide when they want to access the information.

However, if the news is not good, consider how it should be received. With email, the bad news is sent directly to someone's desk without any prior warning. Also, consider how hard it is to gauge how the message will be interpreted. One of the most difficult areas of email communication is getting the tone right. The way in which the email is structured can affect how it is interpreted. For example, factual content set out in short sentences with bullet points will look professional but could be interpreted as abrupt or dictatorial by the recipient.

Format the email to increase the read rate

Subject lines are important in order to achieve the best possible 'read rate'. If the information is a regular progress report, consider giving each of these emails the same subject. However, include in the subject line the date of the report, so that the stakeholders can store them in date order for future reference. If the email is about a specific project achievement, give it a title that gives the recipient a reason to open it. For example, instead of the name of the project in the subject line, 'Find out when X goes live' would be more effective.

Consider from whose email address the message should be sent. After all, a stakeholder is more likely to read an email from their boss than from a project team member whose name they do not recognize.

Clarify how the audience is expected to respond

If you are expecting feedback, be clear how you wish to receive it and identify methods for feedback that are easy for the receiver to comply with. For example, the 'voting' mechanism, which is now standard on many email systems, enables recipients to respond quickly and simply to indicate their support for an initiative, or to indicate their availability for certain dates or times of future

meetings. Sometimes, requesting a 'read receipt' when the recipient opens the email can be helpful in reminding the recipient that the project team want them to read the email. This mechanism cannot achieve more than this, but sometimes that is all that is needed to encourage the recipient to read on.

Ensure the message can be understood

The structure and format of the email is essential in ensuring that recipients not only read the email, but also that they understand the messages that they are being given. There are a few rules that are worth remembering when structuring any email.

- Do not construct the content in report style – i.e. introduction, main body, conclusion – but invert this: conclusion (i.e. most important), then less important core information and finally least important supporting information.
- Make sure the first paragraph has fewer than 30 words. When a reader is confronted with a long and wordy first paragraph, their first instinct is to stop reading completely. Their second instinct (if they stick with the email) is to skim to the next paragraph, until they find something short enough to engage with.
- The rest of the paragraphs should be no more than five lines long, with spaces and bullet points to break up long sentences so that there are no large blocks of text.
- To keep the body of text short, consider hot links to more details instead of a very long email. However, it is worth remembering that today many emails are read on handheld devices, where scrolling onto hot links can be time consuming and a disjointed way to gather information. Therefore, if hot links are being used, make sure that the main body of the text still gets the vital message across, on the good chance that many recipients will ignore the links.

- Good etiquette dictates that capital letters should not be used unless it is for a very specific purpose. In emails, words spelt in capitals are regarded as shouting at the audience, and are likely to be negatively interpreted.
- Lastly, remember that emails are a form of written communication, and are proof that a communication has taken place. This is an advantage and a disadvantage. For example, if users have been given information via emails prior to taking part in a test or trial run, it is not possible for them to deny all knowledge of the instructions. However, the disadvantage is if the communication is more informal and contains opinions or views that are later retracted or changed. It is always worth considering that 'factual' information works well through any written medium, but opinions and views might be better expressed orally, and on a one-to-one basis, where the room for misinterpretation is less.

A.3 CREATING AN EFFECTIVE PROJECT NEWSLETTER

Newsletters are more detailed than emails, and can contain a wide range of news and information, including pictures, and if the newsletter is an online e-zine (electronic magazine) it can include video and audio clips.

Challenges associated with producing newsletters include ensuring that there are sufficient:

- Stories of interest to the readership
- Resources to write the stories, review the content and publish the newsletter.

Unfortunately, due to the scale of newsletters, they can become a project within a project, and take away vital time and resources from the activities of project management. To ensure that this does not happen, consider the following points:

- Decide on the type of content
- Identify the most appropriate production method
- Identify the format most suited to the content.

Decide on the type of content

The cost and time involved in producing newsletters means that it is not usually worth considering segmenting the audience and tailoring the message to their specific needs. Therefore, the information will have to be of a general nature, with as wide an appeal as possible. It is worth undertaking a survey to find out the key issues of most interest to stakeholders at each part of the project lifecycle before developing a newsletter.

Identify the most appropriate production method

A key decision that the project has to take is the mechanism for producing the newsletter. Printed paper copies can be expensive to produce because of the cost of design as well as production and distribution. However, if the stakeholders do not have online access, this might be the only option open to the project. The advantage of printed newsletters is that they can be left in public spaces, including reception and coffee areas, to increase distribution and readership.

It is important to recognize whom the newsletter is aimed at, whilst also recognizing that readership cannot be guaranteed. In common with emails, not everyone will read an electronic version, and in the case of printed copies, they can be read by anyone who sees a copy, even if they have nothing to do with the project.

The structure of the newsletter is important to ensure that the information is read by as many people as possible. Surveys suggest that staff spend less than a minute skimming newsletters, so in common with the structure of project emails, it is worth considering putting headlines and brief descriptions of articles, so that the reader gets a sense of the content, with a hot link to the further article, or more details in the inside pages.

Newsletters give the project team an opportunity to explain areas of the project in depth, or profile certain aspects of the business that will be impacted by the project. It is worth considering if the project team can use the resources of the organization's in-house communications team (if one exists) to produce the newsletter, particularly as many of the stories are likely to be wider than progress on the project.

Identify the format most suited to the content

Everyone likes looking at pictures rather than reading long articles, so wherever possible illustrate the key points with pictures or, if relevant, diagrams. Try to make the articles interesting by including the context of the information and not just the facts. For example, if one of the stories is highlighting the user training that is scheduled to take place the following month, it would be interesting if the experiences of people attending the pilot course could be captured and written up on behalf of everyone else who is due to attend. This will then answer important points such as:

- How long does the training take?
- What time does it start?
- Where is it being held?
- Do I have to bring anything with me?
- Will there be any tests at the end of the training?
- Will a user guide be provided for use back in the workplace?
- How many people will be attending the training at any one time?

If the project is of relatively long duration, it is worth planning several editions of the newsletter in advance so that the information from one newsletter builds on the information from the previous one, which will help

ensure that the newsletter is not packed with content and therefore difficult to read.

Consider having frequent but short newsletters rather than saving everything up for a couple of months, as there is a danger that important news will get lost. A general rule is 'little and often'.

One of the benefits of newsletters is that it demonstrates expertise, knowledge and confidence in the project. Readers will assume that the project is well understood if the project team has taken the time to produce a newsletter about it.

A.4 CREATING A PROJECT BLOG

Weblogs, or blogs as they are commonly known, are an informal 'diary' of thoughts, feelings, opinions and up-to-date information. For a project, blogs can be written by the project manager, project sponsor (subject to other time commitments) or members of the project team.

Blogs are frequently updated, often daily, and therefore readers are likely to return to them frequently. A traditional static website has far fewer changes made on a regular basis, and often requires coding and technical support. However, once the blogging platform has been set up, it is as easy as sending an email. However, the up-to-date nature of blogs means that whoever is responsible for the entries will need to be very disciplined to ensure that entries are made regularly. Any readership that is built up will disappear as soon as the entries dry up.

Advantages of blogs

- A blog can establish the project manager and project team as experts in their field, knowledgeable and confident about what they are trying to achieve. It displays a willingness to communicate and an openness in sharing up-to-the-minute information that will reassure stakeholders.

- A blog can provide a human element to the project, and this can be especially relevant when the project is seeking to implement organizational change affecting the day-to-day work of many employees.
- The posts are usually written in a conversational tone and often contain personal elements about the writer. Those personal elements are where the human face on the project appears. Therefore, whoever is selected to be the author of the blog must be a 'chatty' person – at least 'chatty' via a keyboard if not 'chatty' face to face. This can be an advantage for relatively shy project staff, who would not be comfortable addressing a formal meeting, but are very web aware and familiar with blogs.
- As readers often return daily, they will get to know the author on a more personal level. For example, a project manager might write on their blog about a visit from a possible supplier, and include details that would not normally go in a formal report such as jokey comments that were made by the review team, or things that the project manager discovered, such as the log-on screen was simple to use and could be personalized for each user.
- Blogs usually contain a comments section so reader feedback can be almost instantaneous. Many bloggers will address this feedback in their next posting so blogs are very open. However, for controversial projects it is worth monitoring the tone and contents of comments, as other forms of communication such as one-to-one meetings might need to be held with anyone raising detailed concerns about how the project affects them.

A.5 GIVING AN EFFECTIVE FORMAL PRESENTATION

In some cases, it is necessary for members of the project team (often those who fulfil the role of project manager or project sponsor) to undertake formal presentations or speeches on the state of the project or its impact on the organization. This is an area of communications that can raise concerns as many staff who fulfil vital project roles would not necessarily see themselves as speechmakers.

It is important to consider the following factors when giving any kind of formal presentation:

- Why is the presentation necessary?
- Who is the audience?
- How familiar is the audience with the subject matter?
- What do I want the audience to do with the information being given?

Why is the presentation necessary?

There must be a clear purpose to the presentation. Whilst this might sound obvious, too often a presenter stands up to speak about a project without having any clear idea of the key messages that need to be presented. It is also important to consider why the information being presented is important to be heard at this point in the project lifecycle. Simply standing up and talking about the project in general terms will not guarantee a satisfied audience.

In any presentation, it is vital to demonstrate knowledge of the audience's aims and objectives in turning up to the presentation. Address these in the opening remarks. For example, if the presentation is to provide information that the audience will cascade back to their staff, start by outlining the questions that will be addressed:

> 'I know a lot of staff members have been asking when the project is going to go live, and whether they will need to attend any training before this, particularly as we are getting close to the summer holidays. I am going to explain the five key steps that the project must complete before go live, give you the dates these are likely to be completed by, and what might hold things up, and then go over the training requirements for all levels of staff.'

This outlines a clear purpose, whilst showing empathy for the amount of pressure the audience is under to deliver information to their staff.

Who is the audience?

Consider who the audience is in relation to the speaker. Is the audience a peer group, or is it more senior or more junior than the speaker? The reason for considering this point is that it helps shape the tone of the message that is being given, and the approach that the speaker will need to take.

For example, if the speaker is a relatively junior member of the project team, and is addressing the project sponsor and other senior managers, the tone will need to be deferential at least in part, and any criticisms of operational areas will need to be carefully worded. If the speaker is addressing a peer group or more junior staff, it will be easier to refer to common ground, crack some jokes and take the approach of 'we are all in it together'.

How familiar is the audience with the subject matter?

No audience likes to be patronized, and it shows a lack of planning if the presentation begins with an explanation of information that the audience already knows very well. If the audience has been involved with the project from the start, and is already familiar with key activities, or the reasons why certain suppliers were chosen, do not start with a 10-minute introduction of what the project is about. Get straight to the point and provide new information – which the audience does not already have. However, if the audience has not had any engagement in the project, then the history and an explanation of the key players is helpful and allows the audience to put what is being said into context.

What is the audience expected to do with the information being given?

Formal presentations are too often used as an oral newsletter. Whatever the subject matter, the audience will use the information, even if it is to say to their colleagues what a waste of time the presentation was. Therefore, consider what happens next. Will the audience use the information:

- As a basis for briefing their own staff?
- To undertake work on the project and become contributors?
- To 'set the scene' for external stakeholders such as customers, suppliers and regulators?

A.6   PODCASTS AND VODCASTS

A podcast is an audio broadcast that has been converted to an MP3 file. It can be downloaded from the project intranet site, or can be sent to stakeholders for them to play on their PC or on their iPod. A vodcast is a video broadcast and can be downloaded by stakeholders. These are not two-way forms of communication, so any messages must be general and suitable for all stakeholders, as their distribution cannot be tightly controlled. Therefore, the considerations that apply to newsletters and presentations also apply to podcasts and vodcasts.

A.7   ONE-TO-ONE MEETINGS

In some cases, a broadcast message to all stakeholders does not provide the necessary interaction with the stakeholders most impacted by a project. In this case, a one-to-one meeting is an important communication tool.

Advantages of one-to-one meetings

- As the meeting is private between the stakeholder and the project team, there can be a discussion about confidential or sensitive matters such as the impact on operational staff, the need for redundancies, or the adverse reaction of staff to the proposed changes brought about by the project.

- The stakeholder can raise issues of concern about the project team, including any misunderstandings or aspects of the project that the stakeholder is unhappy about.

In a face-to-face situation, both parties have an opportunity to gain feedback and clarify any misunderstandings, although for this to be fully effective, those holding the meeting must agree some ground rules so that they feel comfortable raising areas of conflict safely and without repercussions. For example, it might be agreed that minutes of the meeting are not taken, or that each party is allowed to complain about the other for five minutes each, followed by 10 minutes to identify actions to rectify the situation. This is always a useful focus, to ensure that, whatever the situation, the meeting results in actions to solve problems and move the project forward towards completion.

A.8 QUESTION AND ANSWER SESSIONS

In order to create an open environment and to reassure staff that the project is not 'working behind their backs' to change the way in which they conduct their roles, senior members of staff involved in the project should have an open dialogue with stakeholders who are impacted by the project.

This open dialogue can take the form of 'road shows' where there is the opportunity for face-to-face engagement, or be via web chats and forums. For web forums, it is important to establish ground rules about the immediacy of the response, who will respond and which questions will be responded to.

A lot of questions can arise during the life of the project on the impact of the project once it has been implemented, and the changes that will result to processes, job responsibilities and reporting lines as a result of this implementation. As questions are received, consider whether answers should be posted within a set time period, and if so, what the most suitable period is so that the answers are current whilst ensuring that providing these answers does not become the dominant project activity.

Confidentiality of questions

In some cases, the answers to questions are sensitive, especially if roles are being removed or changed in some way. Therefore, does the forum promise to reply to all questions or will there be a selection process? For those questions that are not answered, should consideration be given to following up the points raised in some other way, possibly by addressing the business units concerned.

There is definitely a cross-over between project management and operational management in this area of communication, and the project team will need to identify who from the operational area would be best placed to respond to questions, ensuring that they have the authority of senior management to do so.

If no questions or too few questions are being raised, try to discover the reasons for this. If people are hesitant in using any system that is set up, consider using the Issue Log or Risk Log from the project as a source of ideas that can be answered using this forum.

A.9 POSTERS

Posters are static, so whatever message is chosen must be unchanging and remain current throughout the life of the project. Therefore, posters are often a good means of raising awareness of a specific issue – a launch date, contact details for a helpline number or a website address for further information.

For projects that have a long lead time prior to implementation, there are two ways to use a poster campaign. One is to hold back from using them until very close to the end of the project, when awareness of and interest in the project needs to be rekindled prior to the big effort required for implementation. Posters can have an immediacy that is helpful to achieve this.

Factors to consider when planning a poster

- In comparison to email-style communications, posters are relatively expensive to produce because of the design and printing costs, but can have benefits in terms of raising awareness and profile of the project.
- Care should be taken over where the posters will be displayed, which is related to the information that they contain and who they are targeted at.
- Posters work well for projects that impact large numbers of staff and/or impact a significant number of departments across the organization. However, they are only seen by those working in or visiting the buildings in which they are displayed, so have no effect on those working from home or in geographically distant offices.
- As with all project communications, if the stakeholders do not find the posters useful or helpful they will attract criticism. For a poster campaign, the type of criticism received can be along the lines of 'they should get on with the project and stop wasting time telling people how to contact them'. Or stakeholders will question the cost of the poster campaign and wonder what else the money could have been spent on.

A.10 WORKING WITH STAKEHOLDERS

The project team can use a number of methods to work collaboratively with the stakeholders, providing and receiving information in a two-way exchange:

- Workshops
- World café
- Discussion boards.

Workshops

Workshops are a popular term for any event where those attending are expected to participate rather than receive a formal presentation. In a workshop, members of the project team will take on the role of facilitator, where they will help the group achieve the objectives without personally taking any sides of the argument. The facilitator is also responsible for achieving a consensus on any disagreements that arise during the workshop.

To hold a successful workshop, there are a number of important points to consider:

- Number of participants
- Questions to be asked
- Structure of the event
- Handling the results.

Number of participants

The most suitable number of participants will be impacted by the purpose of the workshop, the available accommodation, the type of activities that participants will undertake and the confidence of the facilitator to manage sizeable groups.

During the workshop, participants will be asked for their opinions, but they can also be presented with project issues about which they must agree a way forward. They can also be asked to identify risks that may affect the project, based on their previous experience. Any invitations must clarify the purpose of the workshop and ensure that those being invited have had access to any relevant information that will allow them to take part.

Questions to be asked

The questions that are asked are directly related to the purpose of the workshop. A workshop can be used at any point in the project lifecycle, and the most common uses are:

- **Project initiation workshop** – where the objectives, the scope and the products to be produced by the project are identified. Participants usually represent users who will be impacted by the new products, and suppliers who will be responsible for their design and development.
- **Risk workshop** – where risks are identified and evaluated for their impact and probability of occurrence, and possible responses are identified. By undertaking this work as part of a workshop, ownership and responsibility for the risk responses can be shared across the stakeholders.
- **Quality workshop** – where the standards, quality requirements and methods by which quality will be assessed can be debated and confirmed. By involving a wide range of stakeholders in this workshop, the responsibility for quality management becomes a collective responsibility, rather than being shouldered by only the project team.
- **Lessons learned workshop** – this will occur towards the end of a stage or the end of a project, when all stakeholders can be brought together to identify those aspects of the project that went well and should be repeated in future projects and those aspects that were not successful and must not be repeated.

Structure of the event

In order for participants to become fully involved in the workshop, there is usually the need to provide up-to-date project information. Although this can be provided in written format, in a workshop it is often easier to ask experts and specialists to provide a short presentation on the subject to be discussed, after which the participants can undertake exercises and activities using the information from the presentation.

Typical activities for a workshop include:

- **Discussion groups** – where the participants are divided into small random groups and asked to debate a specific topic, or identify a number of factors, features or benefits about the project. Members of the group are invited to report back to the other participants of the workshop, and the facilitator will guide the presentation, to draw out answers and compare information with the other groups.
- **Solution design** – participants are asked to work with others, in pairs or in small groups, to solve a particular problem. For example, if the project is running late or is over budget, they might be asked to identify parts of the project that can be de-scoped to get the project back on track. The advantage of this type of session to the project team is that there is a collective decision that is made by those who designed the solution, rather than the ideas having to be created by the project team and authorized by the project sponsor.

Room set-up must also be considered. Workshops need more space than a sit-down meeting, because of the need for delegates to move into different groups, and the space required to create presentations, often using whiteboards or flipcharts. Some facilitators feel that there is greater participation if there are no tables in the room, as tables indicate a formality that does not lead to ideas generation. However, if participants require large amounts of written information during the workshop, it is better to have tables and chairs, but in a 'cabaret' style, which means grouping a small number of chairs around each table to create an informal environment.

Handling the results

The facilitator must decide before the event how the information that is developed will be applied to the project. Any goodwill that is generated from holding a workshop can be quickly lost if the participants feel that nothing has been done with their ideas. Immediately after the workshop, the facilitator should thank everyone for coming and set out a timetable for how the information will be applied to the project, and in what format the stakeholders will be able to see the results. For example, there may be a write-up in the project newsletter, or the agreed quality standards will be applied to the next set of reviews that the project is scheduled to carry out.

During the workshop, the facilitator must collect the answers, either by holding onto all flipcharts that are created by the groups, or by taking extensive notes. It is often very difficult to make sense of flipcharts created by others after the event, so it is a good idea to combine these two approaches. However, this makes facilitation of the event itself very difficult as collating feedback is time-consuming; therefore the main facilitator would benefit from assistance from project support in gathering information, ideas and feedback.

World café

This is a method by which conversations are developed between a large number of stakeholders to gather views and ideas on a specific initiative. The conversations are facilitated by one person, who sets the items to be considered and is responsible for gathering all of the information at the close of the session. Key points to consider when using world café are:

- Number of participants
- Questions to be asked
- Structure of the event
- Handling the results.

Number of participants

World café is an effective mechanism for getting ideas from, and exchanging information with, a high number of participants. As there is a need for participants to join different tables for different discussions, there is a relatively high minimum number that will be required, usually 16–20, with the maximum number of participants being as high as several hundred.

As the information being exchanged is in the form of conversations, world café is suitable for all types of participant, whether or not they are well informed about the project. Often, it is the sharing of experiences and information that is the most valuable output, so there is not usually a need to segment stakeholders by role or interest in the project, and there is no need to give out any reference material before the event.

Before invitations are issued, set out a table plan, and identify the most appropriate number of participants per table. If there are few participants per table, the conversations can become stale relatively quickly, but if there are too many, there will be insufficient time for everyone to have their say. Find a suitable venue and calculate how many tables the room can hold – this will determine the maximum number of participants.

Consider inviting more than the maximum number if there is a chance that not all those invited will turn up, and ask for confirmation prior to the event, to ensure that there are enough attendees on the actual day.

In larger groups, it is easier for shy delegates to not participate; in smaller groups, it is easier for one person to dominate the proceedings. Six to eight participants works well, four is too few and more than eight participants can become difficult to manage.

Questions to be asked

The questions are identified once the objectives of the session have been clarified. Questions that the facilitator must ask themselves include:

- Where in the project lifecycle is the project?

■ What are the key issues that have been highlighted by stakeholders to date?

■ Are the stakeholders broadly for or against the project?

■ What are the most relevant subjects to discuss with this group of stakeholders? Relevance can be connected to:

- Responsibilities of the stakeholders to the project
- Expertise or technical knowledge that the stakeholders have
- Impact that the project is likely to have on these stakeholders.

Structure of the event

The room in which world café takes place is set up with a number of chairs grouped around small tables, much like the setting of a café. The tables are laid with paper tablecloths and pens are provided on the table. Small groups of stakeholders take their place at each table, and all of the tables are posed the same question at the same time. Facilitators might want to consider structuring the event so that initial questions are on subjects about which everyone feels immediately confident to contribute, and later questions need a degree of analysis and argument to draw out the information from all, which is easier to achieve when participants understand the process. The event proceeds as follows:

1 A specified amount of time is given to the groups to discuss the question, and all participants are asked to record their ideas, thoughts, opinions and actions on the paper tablecloth.

2 After the set amount of time has expired, some members of the group are asked to join other groups and some of the group are asked to stay where they are.

3 Participants who stay on their original table are responsible for summarizing the discussion they have just had with the stakeholders who join their table for round two.

4 At the end of round two, the process is repeated, with those who previously stayed moving to other tables, and those who joined the original group staying put. Again, the participants who do not move have to summarize the conversation that they have just had.

This can carry on until the facilitator feels that stakeholders have moved a sufficient number of times to create a really integrated community of ideas, and that the ideas relating to the original question have been fully exhausted. At this point, the facilitator can introduce a new question, and repeat the process again, with the advantage that the group is now fully integrated and comfortable with the process and more relaxed about sharing their ideas.

Often, participants relax once they understand the timeframe within which they are asked to consider each question at each table, as they realize that they cannot sit on the sidelines and that they will need to contribute relatively quickly before it is time to move on.

For the facilitator, a real challenge is to plan the room and the number of tables so that there will be sufficient movement of stakeholders to generate as many different conversations as possible. In order for the facilitator to keep control of the event, it is helpful to have worked out in advance how many of each group should remain at the end of each session, and how those that are being asked to move tables should do so. For example:

■ Should 50% of participants remain, or 25% or 75%?

■ Should all participants who are moving tables simply move to the left or the right of their original table, or should they be free to move to any table that they want?

Experience suggests that it is easier if participants are allowed to choose which tables they join for the next session, as too regimented an approach can result in participants concentrating on the process and not on their contribution.

Handling the results

Consideration must be given to how the facilitator will process the results of the output, as this will help guide the structure of the questions. In order to facilitate discussion, questions will need to be open, and participants will add their thoughts to the tablecloths, which can be collected at the end of each question. However, as with the results of all discussions, it can sometimes be difficult to make sense of the words and phrases scribbled by participants in the heat of a discussion.

One way to overcome this problem is for the facilitator to have a number of assistants who roam the room, making notes about what they are hearing, and getting a general understanding of the directions in which the discussions are flowing. At the end of the session, these assistants are responsible for collecting the tablecloths and typing up the results, using their own notes as prompts to structure the feedback. For question two, question three etc., other groups of assistants can repeat the process.

An alternative representation of results can be the display of the tablecloths under each question heading, in a room or corridor where participants and other stakeholders can read the results and feed back their conclusions to the project team.

Discussion boards

Discussion boards are also known as web forums or message boards. They are an online communications mechanism. As a result, the project team must take a decision on the mechanism to enable stakeholders to access the discussion with the decision-makers. Effectively there are two choices – use of:

■ the in-house 'intranet' of the organization
■ the internet.

The decision will be affected by the amount of security required for any project information and the access requirements of stakeholders. External stakeholders usually do not have access to an organization's intranet site.

Advantages of discussion boards

■ They enable stakeholders to participate in discussions about the project, and give them the opportunity to solve problems and answer questions so that not all of the project communication is the responsibility of the project team. This can empower the stakeholders to become more involved in the project.

■ Information can be displayed in chronological order of the postings made by stakeholders or as threaded discussions. Threaded discussions occur as a result of software 'grouping' the different postings under common themes.

■ Threaded discussions allow each stakeholder to understand the overall structure of a conversation: specifically who is replying to whom. Therefore, discussion boards are useful in situations with extended conversations or debates. For example, the project team could start a discussion about the requirements of a particular product in advance of a more formal requirements-gathering exercise. Points raised can then be followed up with the advantage that users/operators already feel involved in the project.

■ There is a subtle appreciation of community in hierarchically threaded systems. As responses have to be made to specific posts, they are also made to specific individuals. Threaded conversations therefore tend to focus the writer on the specific views and personality of the individual being responded to. This occurs less in forums where the latest comment is just inserted into the general pool.

Disadvantages of discussion boards

Discussion boards are not suitable for formal gathering of feedback, because they are based on voluntary involvement of stakeholders, and there is the chance that stakeholders are posting responses because they have a strong feeling that is not representative of all stakeholders.

A.11 RECEIVING FEEDBACK ON THE MESSAGE

A project can use a number of methods to pull in information from the stakeholders:

■ Interviews
■ Focus groups
■ Questionnaires.

Interviews

The purpose of individual interviews is to obtain subjective opinions about the project, probe reactions to information, and gather and test ideas.

Advantages of interviews

■ They are an opportunity for the interviewer to show empathy to the interviewee and work with the interviewee to discuss what actions to take as a result of discovering their views. For example, it is a chance to uncover negative views from stakeholders who have not given any feedback to the broadcast messages from the project, especially where the project team has taken silence as indication that all was well.

■ Interviews solicit information from the interviewee so they are a useful feedback mechanism. However, it is important to identify, prior to the interview, what information is being sought and what will be done with the information once it has been received.

Disadvantages of interviews

■ Interviews are time-consuming and can be a relatively slow method of collecting information compared with questionnaires or votes from an online poll.

■ It is unlikely that large numbers of people can be interviewed; therefore, consideration has to be given to who is selected for interview and the effect that this will have on the project. For example, if only senior managers are selected for interview, junior staff can feel disenfranchised. It is worth considering a vertical slice through the range of stakeholders.

Planning an interview

A number of important factors must be planned for ahead of the interview:

■ Who is to be interviewed?
■ What questions will be asked?
■ Where will the interview take place?
■ How long will the interview last?
■ What will happen to the information that is generated?

Conducting the interview

It is important to put people at their ease, often by exchanging pleasantries and explaining the structure of the interview. For example, thank them for agreeing to be interviewed, explain how long the interview is intended to last, explain how answers will be recorded and who will have access to the information afterwards. This is particularly important if the information being sought is of a sensitive nature, perhaps covering the performance of staff or the level of support that exists for a specific initiative.

Factors to consider when conducting an interview

■ The interview should begin once there is a rapport between the interviewer and the interviewee.

■ Questions should be clear and simple, and it is worth trialling them on friends or colleagues first, so that any misunderstandings about what the question is asking are discovered prior to the interview. This is particularly important when there are a number of interviews to be conducted, as any ambiguity about the meaning of a question can lead to a variety of answers and misunderstandings, making it impossible to compare like with like.

■ Ensure that it is the interviewee who does the majority of the talking. This means that the interviewer should pose the question rather than forcing a response or finishing sentences for the interviewee. A great deal of patience is required by the interviewer, and it is important that the interviewer does not comment on the opinions being expressed, especially not to disagree with them.

■ The interviewer has to show a degree of flexibility during the interview. Keep the list of questions available, but be prepared to probe the interviewee on any other interesting or useful points that they make.

■ Closing the interview requires the interviewer to summarize the main points that have been captured and check with the interviewee that there are no further points that they wish to add. Explain how the information is going to be used, check that the interviewee is happy to be contacted again if there is a need to clarify any of the points and thank them for their time.

Handling the results

Conducting an interview requires the full concentration of the interviewer, listening to answers, preparing the next question in their head, picking up on key points that have been mentioned and incorporating them into the next question so that the conversation 'flows'. Therefore, it is difficult to make comprehensive notes when all of this is happening, especially as humans speak approximately seven times faster than we write.

Consider using an audio or video recorder to capture the interview, and then comprehensive notes can be made at a later point. Failing that, ensure that sufficient time is built in between interviews to review the notes and turn them into a comprehensive record of what was said. Any recording must be with the permission of the interviewee, and it can be helpful to give interviewees a written transcript of the conversation to see if they wish to add any more points after the event.

Focus groups

A focus group is a meeting of a representative sample of stakeholders where opinions and views can be sought.

Advantages of focus groups

■ They are useful for soliciting attitudes to the project and its outputs.

■ They are more time effective than one-to-one interviews. If there are a large number of stakeholders to consider, and interviews would gather information from too small a sample, a focus group can be a useful halfway house between one-to-one interviews and questionnaires.

■ Focus groups can encourage reticent interviewees to share their views, because they are in a group with their peers, which can be less intimidating.

Factors to consider when planning a focus group

■ Any group activity has to be carefully planned, as the group dynamic makes it easier for those involved to steer the conversations to their own agenda.

■ The facilitator must establish the objectives of the focus group, and make the purpose clear in the invitation.

■ The number of points that can be covered will depend on the length of time given to each focus group but a useful rule of thumb is that a minimum of six to eight items gives sufficient range in the subject that the conversations do not stall but 10–12 is the maximum that can be covered before participants become confused over the range of information that they are being asked to comment upon.

- Agree group membership, including the number of participants, and whether they will be from a range of departments, customers or suppliers, or whether they will be from one specific group. Too many participants can make it impossible to capture the views of everyone, and a useful rule is no more than 10 participants.
- Consider the most appropriate route for inviting participants to the focus group.

Questionnaires

Advantages of questionnaires

- Questionnaires are useful for collecting information across a high volume of stakeholders.
- They can be answered anonymously, which gives participants greater freedom to express their views.

Factors to consider when planning a questionnaire

- Although a great deal of time can be saved by using questionnaires in comparison with interviews or focus groups, it is important to ensure that the questionnaire can be completed within a reasonable amount of time. The amount of time and patience that participants will have for completing the questionnaire will relate to their level of participation and interest in the project.
- One technique that can reassure participants that the questionnaire will not take too long is a completion diagram, showing them how much progress has been made and how many questions still remain (Figure A.3). Participants can use this information to assess how much longer it will take to complete the questionnaire. For example, in the diagram, as the participant completes each page or screen of the questionnaire, their progress is highlighted at the top of the page.

- The limited interaction between the person that has set the questions and the participants answering the questionnaire mean that the clarity and the simplicity of the questions are essential.
- It is important that the questions are clearly organized so that there is no confusion about the area of the project that information is being solicited about.
- Thought must be given to the way in which the participant can input their views and answer the questions. If the questionnaire contains open questions, then there must be sufficient space to record their answers. However, the use of open questions must be treated with caution:
  - Participants rarely open up and provide high levels of feedback when confronted with 'a blank piece of paper'.
  - Participation rates for questionnaires based on 'open question' are lower than rates for those based on closed questions.
  - There is also a correlation between the use of open questions and the time to completion for a questionnaire.
- Closed questions can be used effectively for gathering a range of feeling/emotion or strength of feeling by using a scale of 1–3 or 1–5 or high to low etc.

Figure A.3 Tracking questionnaire completion

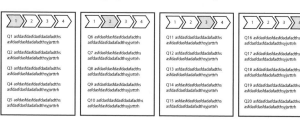

Glossary

Glossary

Activity
An activity is a process, function or task that occurs over time, has recognizable results and is managed.

Baseline
Reference levels against which an entity is monitored and controlled.

Benefit
The measurable improvement resulting from an outcome perceived as an advantage by one or more stakeholders.

Blueprint
A model of the business or organization, its working practices and processes, the information it requires and the technology that will be needed to deliver the capability described in the vision statement.

Business as usual
The way the business normally achieves its objectives.

Business Case
The justification for an organizational activity (strategic, programme, project, operational) which typically contains costs, benefits, risks and timescales and against which continuing viability is tested.

Business change manager
The role responsible for benefits management, from identification through to realization, ensuring the implementation and embedding of the new capabilities delivered by the projects. Typically allocated to more than one individual. Alternative title: 'change agent'.

Capability
A service, function or operation that enables the organization to exploit opportunities.

Communications Plan
A plan of the communications activities during the organizational activity (strategic, programme, project, or operational) that will be established and maintained. Typically contains when, what, how and with whom information flows.

Configuration management
Technical and administrative activities concerned with the creation, maintenance and controlled change of configuration throughout the life of a product.

Customer
The person or group who commissioned the work and will benefit from the end results.

Deliverable
An item that the project has to create as part of the requirements. It may be part of the final outcome or an intermediate element on which one or more subsequent deliverables are dependent. According to the type of project, another name for a deliverable is 'product'.

Executive
The single individual with overall responsibility for ensuring that a project meets its objectives and delivers the projected benefits. This individual should ensure that the project or programme maintains its business focus, that it has clear authority and that the work, including risks, is actively managed. The executive is the chairperson of the Project Board, representing the customer and owner of the Business Case.

Impact
Impact is the result of a particular threat or opportunity actually occurring.

Issue
A relevant event that has happened, was not planned, and requires management action. Could be a problem, query, concern, change request or risk that has occurred.

Issue Log
Contains all project issues including Requests for Change raised during the project. Project issues are each allocated a unique number and are filed in the issue log under the appropriate status.

Opportunity
An uncertain event that could have a favourable impact on objectives or benefits.

Outcome

The result of change, normally affecting real-world behaviour and/or circumstances. Outcomes are desired when a change is conceived. Outcomes are achieved as a result of the activities undertaken to effect the change. In a programme, the outcome is the manifestation of part or all of the new state conceived in the blueprint.

Output

The tangible or intangible product resulting from a planned activity.

Plan

A detailed proposal for doing or achieving something detailing the what, when, how and by whom.

Product

An input or output, whether tangible or intangible, that can be described in advance, created and tested. Also known as an output or deliverable.

Programme

A temporary flexible organization structure created to coordinate, direct and oversee the implementation of a set of related projects and activities in order to deliver outcomes and benefits related to the organization's strategic objectives. A programme is likely to have a life that spans several years.

Programme management

The coordinated organization, direction and implementation of a dossier of projects and activities that together achieve outcomes and realize benefits that are of strategic importance.

Programme manager

The role responsible for the set-up, management and delivery of the programme, typically allocated to a single individual.

Project

A temporary organization that is created for the purpose of delivering one or more business products according to a specified Business Case.

Project Brief

Statement that describes the purpose, cost, time and performance requirements/constraints for a project.

Project lifecycle

The period from the start up of a project to the handover of the finished product to those who will operate and maintain it.

Project manager

The person given the authority and responsibility to manage the project on a day-to-day basis to deliver the required products within the constraints agreed with the Project Board.

Project Plan

A high-level plan showing the major products of the project, when they will be delivered and at what cost. An initial project plan is presented as part of the Project Initiation Document. This is revised as information on actual progress appears. It is a major control document for the Project Board to measure actual progress against expectations.

Project support

An administrative role in the project management team. Project support can be in the form of advice and help with project management tools, guidance, administrative services such as filing, and the collection of actual data. The provision of any project support on a formal basis is optional. Tasks either need to be done by the project manager or delegated to a separate body and this will be driven by the needs of the individual project and project manager.

Risk

An uncertain event or set of events that, should it occur, will have an effect on the achievement of objectives. A risk is measured by a combination of the probability of a perceived threat or opportunity occurring and the magnitude of its impact on objectives.

Risk Log

See Risk register.

Risk Register

A record of identified risks relating to an initiative, including their status and history.

Senior supplier

The Project Board role that provides knowledge and experience of the main discipline(s) involved in the production of the project's deliverable(s). Represents the supplier interests within the project and provides supplier resources.

Senior user

The Project Board role accountable for ensuring that user needs are specified correctly and that the solution meets those needs.

Sponsor

The main driving force behind a programme or project.

Stakeholder

Any individual, group or organization that can affect, be affected by, or perceive itself to be affected by, an initiative (programme, project, activity, risk).

Strategy

The approach or line to take, designed to achieve a long-term aim. Strategies can exist at different levels in an organization – in Managing Successful Programmes there are corporate strategies for achieving objectives that will give rise to programmes. Programmes then develop strategies aligned with these corporate objectives against particular delivery areas.

Supplier

The group or groups responsible for the supply of the project's specialist products.

Team manager

A role that may be adopted by the project manager or senior supplier to manage the work of project team members.

Tranche

A group of projects structured around distinct step changes in capability and benefit delivery.

Transformation

A distinct change to the way an organization conducts all or part of its business.

Index

Index